DIANNE YOUNG

60 THINGS

A Year To Remember

Am sure your 60 Things
will be good reading !!
Happy 60th Fi.
love from The other
Fi X
Bethany
&
Jim

DY

First published by Dianne Young 2020

First edition

ISBN: 978-1-7772801-2-3

Cover art by Olivia Swerhone-Wick

This book was professionally typeset on Reedsy.
Find out more at reedsy.com

To Linda Aksomitis and the other Robins
for giving me the knowledge and the confidence
to publish this book myself.

Contents

Prologue

August 15th

Sixty is not old, right?

When I was a little girl, 60 was *old*! That gray-haired lady that smells like lavender? "I betcha *she's* 60." That bald guy who shuffles along with a walker? "*He's* 60 for sure."

In six months, *I* will be 60.

That little girl still lives in my head, and when I think about my upcoming birthday, she pipes up, "Wow! That's really old!"

Shut it, kid.

Society tries to soften the blow. "Age is just a number." Yeah, but it's getting to be a *big* number.

"Sixty is the new fifty." Sure, just like kale is the new lettuce.

"You're only as old as you feel." Well then, some days I must be 90! The guys from Rice Krispies can't compete with the snaps, crackles and pops my joints produce just getting me out of bed some mornings. But in the spring, on a walk in the park with my dog, Posey—I'm 30. Everything looks fresh, everything smells new and I feel young. In some social situations—like a room full of strangers—I'm 13. "Go introduce yourself," I hear my mother saying, in the back of my mind. "Mo-om!" And if I'm short on sleep, look out—I'm four. "I'm not tired! You're tired! Go away!"

But the calendar says I'll be 60 in six months.

People have started asking, "So what are you going to do for your birthday?" Good question. Moving into a new decade does seem worthy of some kind of celebration. Not just a big party—I did that for my 50th. Maybe a ride in a hot air balloon! I've always wanted to do that. Or a cruise! That would be nice. Or maybe I could learn to play the trombone! How fun would that be! It's so hard to choose just one thing. That's when that little girl pipes up again, "Then do 60 things!"

Hmmm. Not a bad idea, kid. I do like a challenge. If I spread it out over the whole year, that's only five new things a month. Totally doable, and it would certainly be a year to remember!

Okay. The first thing I need to do is to come up with a list—*Things I've Never Done.* I better come up with at least a hundred, so I have some choices. They don't have to be earth-changing, but they might be me-changing, or me-sustaining, or at the very least, fun. I'll go on Facebook—if that doesn't signal that I'm old, I don't know what does—and ask my friends for suggestions. I'm sure they'll come up with some doozies, because trust me, if you think *I'm* weird, you should meet my friends!

Sixty is not old. Not too old anyway. So, to misquote Bette Davis—"Fasten your seatbelts. It's going to be a bumpy *year*!"

But in a good way.

November 15th

Three months to go.

My list is complete! My friends did indeed come up with some amazing suggestions:

- ride an elephant
- go parasailing
- get a tattoo

Also some terrible ones:

- create a new recipe—I have enough trouble following existing ones.
- drive a race car—I once punched out the back window of my parents' little truck by backing into a balcony. I don't think me and excessive speed would be a good mix.
- ride a mechanical bull—Do they even still have those? But even if they do, I'm not athletic enough to ride it at normal speed and not sexy enough to ride it at slow speed.

Some that I've already done:

- go whitewater rafting
- learn to hula hoop
- fly a glider

And some that I will *never* do:

- steer riding
- bungee jumping

- motorcycling

But all in all, I think it's a pretty awesome list.

100 Things I've Never Done

1. Go on a hot air balloon ride
2. Go on a cruise
3. Learn to play the trombone
4. Play a harp
5. Drive a combine
6. Drive a snowmobile
7. Drive a Jet Ski
8. Travel in a truck camper
9. Write a poem in a foreign language
10. Compose a piece for handbells
11. Shave my head
12. Dye my hair
13. Get a facial
14. Get a manicure
15. Get my eyebrows threaded
16. Get a tattoo
17. Celebrate my birthday in the summer
18. Volunteer at the Friendship Inn
19. Make a souffle
20. Eat a frog's leg
21. Eat marijuana-infused chocolate
22. Eat sashimi
23. Eat a raw oyster
24. Eat haggis
25. Have my fortune told

26. Go wall climbing
27. Rappel down a building
28. Do a tandem parachute jump
29. Try axe throwing
30. Try fencing
31. Try lawn bowling
32. Learn to juggle
33. Learn to ride a unicycle
34. Try a pogo stick
35. Try downhill skiing
36. Try snowboarding
37. Try paddleboarding
38. Try tubing
39. Try scuba diving
40. Ride a Crazy Carpet down sand dunes
41. Do a chin-up
42. Try folk dancing
43. Try clogging
44. Try geocaching
45. Play blackjack at a casino
46. Participate in a fishing derby
47. Pan for gold
48. Attend a sweat lodge
49. Attend a pow wow
50. Attend a Jewish worship service
51. Attend a Muslim worship service
52. Attend a Buddhist Meditation class
53. Attend a silent retreat
54. Attend a nudist camp
55. Attend a sing-along movie
56. Attend a bluegrass festival

57. Attend a lacrosse game
58. Attend Folkfest
59. Attend Taste of Saskatchewan
60. Milk a goat
61. Drink a martini
62. Drink green beer on St. Patrick's Day
63. Smoke marijuana
64. Take a stained glass class
65. Take an anti-gravity class
66. Take an aerial yoga class
67. Take a tai chi class
68. Take a belly dancing class
69. Take a drawing class
70. Take a tap-dancing class
71. Learn to swim the butterfly
72. Learn German
73. Learn to skip Double Dutch
74. Ring church bells
75. Get an acupuncture treatment
76. Get a reflexology treatment
77. Float in a sensory deprivation tank
78. Float in Little Manitou Lake
79. Go skinny dipping
80. Go to a nude beach
81. Ride an elephant
82. Ride on a dog sled
83. Ride on a chuckwagon
84. Go hang gliding
85. Go paragliding
86. Go parasailing
87. Go sailing

88. Visit Hawaii
89. Visit Alaska
90. Visit the Yukon
91. Visit Waskesiu
92. Visit the Crooked Trees
93. Visit the Beechy sandcastles
94. Visit the Remai Modern Art Gallery
95. Visit Government House
96. Visit Motherwell Homestead National Historic Site
97. Visit the Saskatchewan Burrowing Owl Interpretive Centre
98. Go on an underground mine tour
99. Sign up on a dating site
100. Go on a blind date

January 15th

One month to go—and I'm having second thoughts. "What was I thinking? I can't do this! This was a terrible idea!"

But after nearly 60 years, I've learned a trick or two about how to manage my fears. If I really want to do something, I know I need to declare it out loud to others. When I first decided to try writing for children, I announced it in the staff room at work, "My New Year's Resolution is to write a children's book." And I did it. When I decided to take an online Calculus class because I had failed it so miserably 40 years ago, I announced it on my blog. And I did it. So, five months ago when I decided to do 60 new things in a year to celebrate my 60th birthday, I announced it at work, and on my blog, and on Facebook. No take-backsies!

Oh, no. This is a bad idea. You can't do this! That would be Ennaid nattering in my ear. She's my annoying inner critic, my nay-sayer, my wet blanket. We all have an Ennaid.

But that's actually a big help, Ennaid. Thanks! If there's anything that spurs me on to do something I'm not sure about, it's someone telling me I *can't* do it—I'm mature that way. Even if that someone is me. *Especially* if that someone is me.

One month to go.

I can do this, right?

February 15th

Happy birthday to me! I can't believe I'm 60. I don't feel 60, or at least I don't feel like I used to think 60 must feel like—thank goodness.

Let the adventures begin!

I

The Adventures

#1 - Shave My Head

February 15th

I wanted to start out with a bang, so I decided the first thing I was going to do was shave my head.

I've always wanted to feel what it would be like to have no hair. Thankfully, I've never had to find out through chemotherapy or for other medical reasons. But I really wanted to know!

I knew this was going to be #1 when I first started making my list. But I didn't tell anyone. Other than my mom—I've been telling her every week for months now. But she has dementia which, for her, means her short-term memory is shot, so I knew she wouldn't remember long enough to tell anyone else. (You can either cry about it, or you can learn to live and laugh with it.)

"You are not! Why would you do that?" I enjoyed her reaction each and every time.

But I also knew I was going to need help. How would I shave the back of my head without losing a pint of blood in the process? Enter my niece, Amber. A few months back she phoned me up to see if I wanted to go on a two-day quilting retreat at a local fabric store with her. It was on my birthday weekend, and if we decided to go, could she stay with me? Perfect!

"Sure! But you have to help me with something for my birthday after the first day of quilting, okay?"

"Help you with what?" she asked suspiciously. She knows me well.

"I can't tell you."

"You're scaring me."

"No, no. Nothing to be scared of. It's going to be awesome!"

"Now I'm really scared."

But she reluctantly agreed. She made a few guesses, "Male strippers? Dyeing your hair green?" but I was certain she would never figure it out.

After a day of quilting, we came back to my place and had supper. I had gathered all the supplies ahead of time—scissors, electric clippers, shave gel, razors—and hidden them in a bag on the counter. After supper, I took out my phone and got her to take a picture of me. Then I got out the scissors.

"Here we go!" I announced with maniacal glee. I gathered up a handful of hair and began to chop it off with the scissors.

"Aaaaa! What are you doing? Stop!" she hollered. I just laughed.

"I'm going to shave my head and you're going to help me!" I continued to grab and chop hunks of hair.

"Why? This is crazy! You're insane!" Her voice had risen an octave in the last ten seconds.

"It's my birthday present to myself!" *Chop.* "I have always wanted to do this." *Chop.* "And since I've never done it before, it's the first thing on my 60 Things list." *Chop.* "Haven't you ever wondered what your head would feel like if it was bald?"

"No! Never! Not ever! I can't do this!" Exclamations seemed to be her only mode of speech at this point.

"Sure you can! I'd look pretty silly if I stopped now!" *Chop.*

Then I got out the electric clippers. She got out her phone—to message my sister and send her pictures of what was going down. Not sure if she thought my sister could talk me out of it or if she just needed to alert someone that she was doing this under duress. Shaking her head, she took the clippers from me and switched them on. *Bzzzzzz!* I could not help but grin as my hair hit the floor. This was awesome! Amber, meanwhile, was trying not to hyperventilate.

"You're doing great!" I cheered her on. She just groaned.

When she was done with the clippers, I ran my hand over my buzzed head.

"That is so cool!" I was like a kid with a new toy.

Next, I squirted the shave gel into my hand and spread it all over my noggin.

"I'm not sure how much of this I need. How's that?" I asked.

"Just peachy!" I detected a note of sarcasm. "I can't believe you're doing this! I can't believe *I'm* doing this!" No sarcasm there.

And so, with a bowl of water and a couple of disposable razors, she began to shave my head. I couldn't wait to see how it would feel!

She did a great job. I slowly ran my hand all over my head. Totally smooth.

"Awesome!" It was my turn to only be able to speak in exclamations. "I love it! Thank you!"

"I'm exhausted," was all she could say, as she took my "After" photo.

I went and had a shower right away, with the excuse that I should wash off all the little hairs and bits of gel that might be stuck on my head—but really, it was just so I could feel the water on my bald head. And run my hand over it again and again. I was giggling. It was amazing!

Even the little girl inside me was enjoying this one!

Ennaid wasn't speaking to me.

Would I do it again?

No. It could never be as great a second time. But I am so glad I did it. A birthday I will certainly never forget!

#2 - Float in a Sensory Deprivation Tank

February 19th

My only experience with a sensory deprivation tank was from an old episode of *Hawaii Five-O*—the original one, with Jack Lord. Wo Fat, Steve McGarrett's arch enemy, had captured Steve and put him in one as torture, to make him reveal state secrets. And now people *pay* to go in them! Sign me up!

I booked my 90-minute session at Float Saskatoon. The "before you come" instructions they gave me were:

- don't shave the day before—you're floating in very very salty water, so floating is unavoidable but stinging isn't
- eat something half an hour before—so your stomach isn't gurgling the whole time
- show up ten minutes early—for instructions

Check, check and check.

When I arrived, I watched an orientation video on a tablet. Then the staff person took me to my room, and ran through the info again:

- ear plugs to wear—and take home as a souvenir, or to use again next time
- how to open the door to the tank—it reminded me of a walk-in cooler except the water and the air were nice and warm
- where the light switch was inside—to shut off once you're in, or leave on if you prefer
- a robe, if you needed to use the washroom at some point—No Peeing in the Pool! They didn't actually say that, but duh!
- where the washroom was
- a little vial of vinegar to squirt in your ears after in case you did get some salt water in them
- a little pillow for your head, if you chose to use it—I didn't

Then she left. I locked the door, got naked and showered. It was dark in the room, with just a deep blue light on, and the air was warm. I opened the door to the tank. The door was about 1 m by 1 m (3 ¼ ft by 3 ¼ ft). Inside there was another blue light. I stepped into the warm salty water. It was only 33 cm (13 in) deep. I closed the door behind me, lay down in the water and shut off the light. Total blackness. Closing my eyes or leaving them open looked exactly the same. My lady bits stung a little bit at first, but only a little. No music playing or anything, just quiet. The floating was effortless. I was a bit like a ping pong ball at first, gently bumping into one wall then the other until I settled and stayed in the centre. And then I relaxed. I was so relaxed I fell asleep at least a few times.

The 90 minutes went by quickly. I thought it would seem like forever, but before I knew it, soft music began to play and the blue light came on again. It was a shame to get out, especially as I thought of the cold awaiting me outdoors back in the real world. But I exited the tank—without revealing any secrets!—showered and dressed, put my souvenir earplugs in my pocket, and returned to the front lobby. There, I had a complementary cup of lemon tea as I lounged on the comfy sofa, and chatted with another woman who had also just finished her float. Then I paid and left. I even got a birthday discount! Nice!

Would I do it again?

It's not something I would do on a regular basis, but as a birthday treat, I could definitely see myself going back.

#3 - Get My Eyebrows Threaded

February 21st

I would describe my eyebrows as two large caterpillars about to attack each other. When I was in my 20s, I would pluck them, but haven't bothered with that for years. My hairdresser, Tracy, the owner of Infinity Salon and Spa, trims them when I get a haircut, but other than that, I leave them alone. Having them threaded was definitely a new experience for me.

I sat in a reclining chair and Rachel, who is Tracy's daughter, brushed my eyebrows in preparation for threading. She took a long piece of thread, doubled it between her fingers, and twisted it. She laid the threads along my eyebrow, her fingers moved and yank! I felt a row of hairs being ripped out. A little ouchy, but no worse than plucking—if I remember correctly—and definitely faster. After Rachel did the tops of my brows, I had to put one hand above my brow and pull up, and the other on my eyelid and pull down, to tighten the skin so she could do the bottom of the brow. Then ditto for the other brow. Rachel threaded away until she was satisfied that both caterpillars were tamed and back in their corners. There were a few granddaddy hairs that felt like their roots were as long or longer than the actual hair, but the pain was still not unbearable. I forgot to check what time we started, but I think it took around 20 minutes all together.

Because I couldn't actually see what was going on, I checked out a video on YouTube afterwards to see how threading works. I learned it's an ancient technique that originated in Iran. The thread ends are knotted together to form a loop. Then the loop is twisted five or six times to form a figure eight. The unwanted hairs are caught in the open spot on one side of the twist, then the other side of the twist is opened, moving the twist over the hairs and yanking them out. Who figures these things out? And how?

Would I do it again?

Sure—in another 60 years!

Update on #1 (one week)

February 22nd

The smooth bald head only lasted one day! Who knew hair grew so fast? In just one week, my head went from smooth, to sandpaper, to Velcro, to velvet (smooth one way but rough the other). It's 0.3 cm (1/8 in) long after only one week. At that rate, it will be 15.6 cm (6 1/2 in) after a year!

#4 - Visit the Remai Modern Art Gallery

February 28th

I'll admit right off the top—I'm not really a fan of modern art. But Saskatoon has a new art gallery, the Remai Modern, so I thought I would check it out. My friend, Cathrin, had never been either, so she joined me for this adventure.

I appreciated that they have a coat room with free lockers that you can put your stuff in and enter your own code to lock, so you don't have to carry your coat around with you. Practicality at an art gallery—colour me surprised.

It's actually a beautiful building, inside and out—modern-looking with big walls of windows and really high ceilings. Very classy. Hanging from the ceiling were cubes made of white venetian blinds. It looked beautiful, and I didn't realize it was actually a piece of art until I read about it on the website later. It's by Haegue Yang and called *Four Times Sol LeWitt Upside Down—Version Point to Point.* (Snappy title, Haegue.)

The first installation we visited was *Tomorrow is the Question* by Rirkrit Tiravanija. It was four ping pong tables in a room. Each table had the words TOMORROW IS THE QUESTION on it in a different colour. There were also paddles and balls for each table, so you could actually play! Which we did. Truthfully, the most fun I've ever had at an art gallery.

After playing ping pong for a while, we headed up the staircase to see the other works of art. First the Canadian gallery. Lots of representations of lady bits and man bits. Not my cup of tea, but some striking colours.

My favourite pieces were definitely the William Perehudoff ones. Probably because they once adorned the walls of Intercontinental Packers, the meat-packing plant where I once worked, and where I met my late husband, Bill. Perehudoff painted scenes on canvas of people working in the plant, as well as pieces representing the arts on the walls of the office reception area. When the building was slated to be demolished, some very smart people arranged for the paintings to be saved by having them stripped from the plant walls and then applied to walls in the new gallery—an amazing process.

If a piece of art sticks with you, even if it's upsetting, I think the artist has accomplished something. The one that stuck with me was *blood on the snow* by Rebecca Belmore. It was a large white quilt-like blanket on the floor that looked like a field of untouched snow. In the centre was a white chair, that looked like it was covered in snow as well. But the top of the back of the chair was deep crimson, like it had been drenched in blood. It was meant to represent the massacre of Indigenous people at Wounded Knee in 1890. Horrifying, but I couldn't look away.

There is also a theatre, in which a short film called *Volcano Saga* by Joan Jonas was playing. It loops over and over throughout the day. Cathrin and I sat and watched it for a while. Tilda Swinton was in it. It was bizarre. We moved on.

Another room contained linocuts and other pieces by Pablo Picasso, as well as a giant photo of him sitting in his studio. I always like seeing the spaces that creators work in. My favourite pieces of his were two bird-shaped ceramic pitchers.

I am not going to get caught up in any debates on what is or isn't art—if the artist says it is, so be it. Some things I liked and some I didn't.

Would I do it again?

Yes, because the exhibits change. I think I would check online first to see what's new, but it's always worth a trip for the memories of Intercon.

#5 - Get an Acupuncture Treatment

March 7th

My friend, Lynn, raves about acupuncture, but I had questions.

"Does it hurt? Do you have to have something that needs fixing?" I asked.

"No and no. It's good for your overall health," she answered. Great!

Leni runs Neil Clinic Acupuncture out of her condo. Lynn has known her since childhood and highly recommended her.

I filled out a short questionnaire online before my appointment. When I arrived, I followed the signs that led me to the back door, inside and down the stairs.

Leni met me at the bottom of the stairs, introduced herself and welcomed me. She was very friendly, and I could see why Lynn liked her.

Leni explained what we would be doing that day. "Before every treatment I do a scan of the client's energy using this metal wand that is hooked up to my computer." The wand had a damp Q-tip stuck in the end of it which she touched to different points on my hands and feet. Then we looked at the resulting bar graph.

About half of the bars were green—which is what you want—and most of the rest were red, with a couple of purple thrown in as well.

"Like most people who have never had acupuncture, you have a Belt Block," she explained. "The energy isn't flowing through your body as it should, but is getting stuck in your middle."

"Sounds like energy has a lot in common with fat," I joked.

Next, I lay down on my back on a massage-type table and Leni showed me the needles she would be using. They were very thin, single-use, and sterile.

"To open up your Belt Block, I will be inserting four needles—one in each foot and one in each forearm." I really liked that she explained each step. I could feel the needles going into my feet—not pain, but more like heat. I couldn't feel the ones going into my arms at all.

"We'll leave the needles in for 20 minutes," she said. "I'll turn down the lights and you can relax, sleep, chat, whatever you like. I'll be right here at my desk." So of course, I chatted. I asked her all about when and how she got into acupuncture, where she took her training, and how she knew Lynn. The 20 minutes went by quickly. She's a really interesting woman.

Would I do it again?

Yes, I would. In fact, before I left, I booked an appointment for another treatment next week.

Update on #5

March 8th

One day after my acupuncture treatment, I had so much energy, it was ridiculous! Whenever I have a Reiki treatment I always feel energized, but this was like a super-boost! I could honestly feel the energy flowing through my arms. I got so much done! And my mind was racing with creative possibilities. It was almost to the point of having too much energy! I felt even more fidgety than usual—I have difficulties with sitting still. Leni told me later that this super energy boost sometimes happens, but that it's a one-time first-time experience. Too bad!

#6 - Start Learning German

March 11th

I love Duolingo. It's a free language-learning app I used a couple of years ago to learn enough Spanish to get by in Mexico. I actually love learning languages—it's like a secret code. Yep, I'm nerdy that way.

There are currently 33 different languages you can choose to learn on Duolingo, including Klingon (for *Star Trek* fans) and High Valyrian (for *Game of Thrones* fans). I've decided I'm going to start learning German. Wish me *Glück*!

Would I do it again?

It will be an ongoing project, but I could definitely see myself using this program to learn other languages in the future. It's fun!

Update on #1 (one month)

March 15th

It's been one month since I shaved my head. Just to recap, the stages have been: baby bum bald, sandpaper, Velcro, velvet and then after about three weeks—duckling! I couldn't stop running my hand over my head—ooooh, so soft!

I had my friend, Betty Lou, measure it with a ruler today and it's 1 cm (3⁄8 in) long. Either the growth has slowed down, or I've worn 0.3 cm (1⁄8 in) off by rubbing it so much in the duckling stage—ooooh, so soft! But even if it only grows 1 cm (3⁄8 in) per month, that's still 12 cm (4 1⁄2 in) in a year.

But the duckling stage is over. Now it just feels like hair. Kind of sad.

#7 - Try Axe Throwing

March 15th

Apparently axe throwing is a thing now, so I decided to give it a try. I booked a one-hour slot at Timberjaxe for myself and five friends—Betty Lou, Barb and Ross, and Erin and Murray. After signing a waiver that basically says no matter what happens it's not their fault, a worker led us to our area. The floor and back wall of each throwing area is made of wooden planks. There is floor-to-ceiling chain-link between each area, and two big wooden targets on the back wall. We were shown the different sizes of hatchets, and how to throw them, both overhand and underhand, and then were left to it. Two people could throw at a time. We all started with the classic overhand throw, but it took a while before anyone managed to have one stick in a target. Murray was the first, but we eventually all got it. It gives a very satisfying *thunk* when you do it right. Betty Lou preferred the two-handed over-your-head technique.

Then we tried underhand. Oh my. The worker had warned us, "The first time you try it, it will probably go high."

That was an understatement. The planks on the back wall end about 4.5 m (15 ft) up, and on my first underhand attempt

I managed to throw a hatchet up onto that ledge! Oops. And there it stayed for the rest of the evening, taunting me. Again, with practice, almost everyone stuck at least one underhand throw.

Next up was two-at-a-time overhand—one hatchet in each hand. Barb made it look easy. I made it look impossible. But I persevered and eventually—ta da!—I got both hatchets to stick. I definitely wanted a picture of that. But on my way to the target, one of them fell out! I tried chopping it back in, but no dice. And do you think I could do it again? No. I tried and I tried, but my two-hatchet victory would have to remain proof-less. Oh well, *I* know I did it.

Would I do it again?

Sure. Lots of misses, lots of laughter, and lots of fun. And good to know for next time—if you bring your own hatchet, you get 15% off!

#8 - Try Scuba Diving

March 17th

I signed up for a Discover Scuba class a couple of weeks ago. George, the instructor, told me there would be about 45 minutes of instruction at the shop and then we would head to Harry Bailey Aquatic Centre for an hour of practice. I've been looking forward to it ever since!

I showed up at the shop, The Saskatoon Diving Center, a few minutes early, which was good because, in my excitement, I had forgotten to fill out the waiver that George had given me when I signed up. It's basically to check for any medical conditions that might not allow you to participate. I passed.

I was the only one signed up for the class that night. First off, George took me upstairs to watch a video that explained:

- the parts of the equipment
- how to move underwater—you don't use your arms, just your legs
- how to equalize the pressure in your ears as you descend
- the underwater hand signals
- some safety measures—like how to find the regulator and

replace it if it comes out of your mouth underwater and how to empty water out of your mask underwater

Once the video was over, George went over the information with me again, which was good because there was a lot and I'd already forgotten some of it. Then we left for the pool.

The pool is closed to everyone else during scuba lessons, so you don't have to worry about swimming into people or having people jump on you. I met George on the deck and he got someone to help me find a mask and fins while he got a tank ready for each of us. We sprayed some defogger in our masks, rubbed it around and rinsed it off in the pool. Sitting on the edge of the pool, I put on my gear—fins, a BCD (Buoyancy Control Device), a tank, and a mask, and then slid into the water. The BCD is an inflatable vest that prevents you from getting pulled down by your tank when you want to float at the surface.

We were in the shallow part of the deep end and the first thing George got me to do was to stick my head underwater and breathe. No problem! Then he went over the safety measures again and got me to try them. Success! We were ready to descend.

Easier said than done. I had a heck of a time getting stable—I was either floating up too much or sinking down. George was trying to help me by adjusting my BCD but finally he motioned to head back up to the shallow end. He went over technique again, and I gave it another shot. I figured it out the second time around.

For the next half an hour or so, I swam around the bottom of the pool. It was kind of cool. Until I started feeling sick. (I found out later that motion sickness is common in new divers.) I headed up to the surface and to the edge of the pool, hoping

I wouldn't puke into the regulator. Yuck! I didn't. And I felt a little better at the surface. George came to check on me and I explained I was feeling nauseous, so we called it quits. We only had a few minutes to go anyway. An interesting evening, even if it did end with an upset stomach.

Would I do it again?

Probably not. I'm glad I tried it, but I didn't really like the feeling of pressure and the noise of the bubbles. Of course, it might be different if you were looking at tropical fish instead of the bottom of a public swimming pool, but I think I'll stick to snorkeling.

Update on #6 (one week)

March 18th

Guten Tag! *I've been learning German for a week now and I'm having a blast.*

I've learned that, in German, nouns are always capitalized, but the pronoun "I" (ich) *is not. My favourite German word so far?* Entschuldigung, *which means "sorry." How Canadian of me!*

#9 - Go to a Rush Game

March 30th

I went to a party and a lacrosse game broke out—okay, fair warning, this report is going to make me sound like a grouchy old lady. Saskatoon has had a professional lacrosse team, the Saskatchewan Rush, since 2015. I invited my friends, Debbie and Dave, to go with me. Both their sons played lacrosse, so I figured they could explain things to me.

It was not what I expected.

It was quite a production, that's for sure. But to me, it seemed about 25% sporting event and 75% distraction. Fireworks, flashing lights—they even have their own DJ, and music is pumping the entire time. A lot of the people sitting around us didn't seem to be paying much attention to the game, except for when the Rush scored. Then they would scream and yell, and go through a routine of beating their right fist over their heart. Some people added raising their right arm straight up in the air at the end of that. I copied the chest-beating sometimes, but sorry—any kind of straight arm "salute" kind of creeps me out.

You could hardly tell if the other team scored, unless you

actually saw the goal—which since a lot of people weren't actually watching the game, wasn't likely—or you noticed the score change on the clock. No groans from the crowd, no sighs—there seemed to be no reaction at all. Weird.

The game itself was fast-paced and interesting—lots of passing, lots of running, and a 30-second shot clock. A team has to take a shot on net within 30 seconds or the other team gets the ball. It was also fairly physical, although not as much body-checking as hockey, I would say.

And unfortunately, there were fights. (The only sport that throwing punches is "part of the game" to me, is boxing.) But the crowd loved it. *Cringe.* There were three fights at the game that night—two on the field and one in the stands by us. Needless to say, alcohol was involved.

The Rush won the game, by the way.

Would I do it again?

I would go to a lacrosse game again, but not to a Rush party—I mean, game. I did find out later that our seats were in the notorious party corner, and that most people *do* watch the game. But still, I'd prefer it without all the loud music and hype—told you I'd sound like a grouchy old lady.

#10 - Get My Hair Dyed

April 1st

I stopped in to see Tracy last week to ask if my hair was long enough to dye. Since I'd never done it before, I didn't know if it had to be a certain length.

"Sure it is!" she said.

"Awesome! Book me in."

"How about next Monday? April first."

"April Fool's Day? One of my favourite days of the year. Perfect!"

When I returned on Monday, Tracy washed and dried my hair, then got out the colour book.

"What colour are you thinking?"

"Purple!" I said, grinning.

There are a few reasons I went with purple:

- I wrote a children's book that was published in 1994 called *Purple Hair? I Don't Care!*
- If it's purple, I hope people will think, "Oh my! She has purple hair!" instead of what many of them think now when they see me with my super-short hair,"Oh my! I bet

she has cancer!"

- Because it's so short, it will grow out quickly and maybe then just the ends will be purple, which would also be cool.
- Go big or go home, right?

Tracy knows me. I don't think she was even surprised. "Okay, and what shade of purple?"

"Bright purple!"

"I figured as much. How about this?" She showed me a tube of bright purple dye.

"Perfect!"

Step one was to bleach my hair. Tracy painted the bleach on with a brush and then I sat for 20 minutes or so to let it work. It wasn't even smelly! The result was very blonde hair on the sides and orangish hair on top. Cool!

Then came the purple. I couldn't stop grinning as Tracy painted it on. Another 20 minutes of sitting, a good rinsing, and ta-da!—*Purple Hair? I Don't Care!* Wait till my mom sees this!

Would I do it again?

No. I love that I did it, but from now on, the colour that it grows out of my head is the colour it will be.

#11 - Get a Manicure

April 4th

I had a pedicure once—a friend gave me a gift card for one—but I'd never had a manicure. So, I called Tracy again, and set up an appointment.

I do not take care of my nails. I do not really even notice them, other than to keep them clean. It just has never been a thing with me. My nails grow. I let them. They get long and annoy me—especially when they click on the keys while I'm playing the piano—then I rip them off. I tried nail polish a few times when I was younger, but didn't have the patience for it.

"Do you want polish or shellac?" Tracy asked.

"What's the difference?"

"Shellac lasts longer."

"Sounds good. Shellac it is."

She brought out the colour book, and I picked a bright red with sparkles in it. Why not?

First, she pushed back my cuticles, and trimmed them. I thought that part would hurt—I seemed to remember it did when *I* tried it—but it didn't. Then she filed my nails and sanded them to remove the ridges. Ridges in your nails are just another "perk" of growing older.

Tracy applied five coats of stuff to my nails—a sealer, a builder, two coats of shellac and a glossy top coat. After each coat, except for the sealer, I put my hand in a little machine with an LED light in it—to cure the coat. It didn't take long at all. And despite them being perfectly dry, I would still catch myself holding my fingers apart for the next hour or so.

Would I do it again?

No. Again, it was fun to do once, but I can think of better ways to spend my time and money.

#12 - Take a Belly Dancing Class

April 5th

I googled belly dancing and found an instructor in Saskatoon named Anastasia. I emailed her and asked about having just one lesson for me and a group of friends and she was happy to set it up.

"Who wants to try belly dancing with me?" I put the call out quickly—before Ennaid could talk me out of it—and six friends signed on in no time: Barb and Erin (my axe throwing friends), Cathrin (my gallery visiting friend), Karen, Lynn, and Marilyn. I have the best friends.

We met Anastasia downtown at the Dance Saskatchewan studio. She supplied us with jingly scarves to tie around our hips. I chose purple, of course, to match my hair.

First we lined up in two rows before a wall of mirrors. A wall of mirrors? And the laughter began.

"Bummer! I thought only *other* people would have to watch me."

Anastasia was a great teacher. We'd learn each move slowly, then speed it up, and then add on another move. The moves and our running commentary went something like this:

- stepping forward and back

"Aargh! How is *this* hard?"
"I gotta stop looking in the mirror. It's messing me up."

- washing-machine hips (without moving your upper body, alternate pushing each hip bone forward)

"I think my washing machine is broken."
"Know any good repairmen?"

- side-stepping one way then the other with some arm movements thrown in

"Oh-oh. We're adding arms?"
"I'm obviously coordinationally-challenged."

- turning diagonally and alternately sticking out one hip and pointing the opposite foot forward. Then shuffling to the other diagonal and repeating with the other hip and foot

"I didn't realize belly dancing would make my brain hurt!"
"Wait until tomorrow. Everything will hurt then!"

- shoulder rolls, hip rolls and boob lifts (basically sticking out your boobs without raising your shoulders)

"Why does my body refuse to do what my brain is telling it to do?"
"I can't even think anymore!"

- and of course, the shimmy

"Woohoo! Ring those jingles, ladies!"
"This is the best!"

At the end of the class, each row did the routine for the other row. I thought we were all awesome! So much laughter, so much fun.

Would I do it again?

I'm not much of a dancer, so probably not, but I was glad I tried it.

Update on #6 (one month)

April 11th

It's been one month since I started learning German. It's going great! The word "the" is driving me a little crazy though—should it be der *or* das *or* die *or* den*? It seems to depend on a lot of things, so it's easiest just to learn what goes with what and when. For instance:* Apfel *means"apple." If you want to say "the apple," as in "the apple is red," it's* der Apfel. *But if you want to say "the apple," as in "I ate the apple," it's* den Apfel. *And if there is more than one apple, it's* die Äpfel. *Which brings me to plurals—you don't just add an "s" in German. Sometimes the word itself doesn't even change, just the "the."* Das Mädchen *means "the girl."* Die Mädchen *means "the girls." Eventually, I'll get the hang of it.*

New favourite words? Schmutzig, *which means "dirty", and* schmeckt, *which means "tastes".* Der Apfel schmeckt gut!

#13 - Play the Harp

April 18th

I have loved the sound of the harp since I was a child watching *Friendly Giant* on TV. If you've never heard of the show, there was a giant (Friendly) and a talking rooster puppet (Rusty) and a talking giraffe puppet (Jerome). Every episode, Friendly would read a picture book to Rusty and Jerome (and me), or have a concert with the help of two cat puppets or two raccoon puppets. Friendly played the recorder. I liked the episodes when he read a book the best.

The show began with Friendly talking about what was going on in the little village or farmland around the castle as the camera panned across a miniature scene. Then the camera would stop when it came to a giant boot, and Friendly would always say, "There's that big boot. Now look up, waaaay up (the camera would pan up to his face) and we're on our way to the castle. I'll hurry over first and go in the back door so I can let the drawbridge down and open the big front doors for you. Are you ready? Here's my castle." A harp would then play beautiful magical-sounding glissandos and the camera would cut to a shot of the front of the castle. As the camera slowly zoomed in on the drawbridge, the harp would be joined by a recorder and they would play the theme song, "Early One Morning." I loved that show.

When I found out my friend, Pat, actually *played* the harp, I crossed my fingers and asked her if she would let me try it sometime. Maybe give me a mini-lesson? Bless her heart, she said, "Sure!"

I was so excited, I had butterflies in my stomach the day I went to her house. Her harp is about 1.6 m (5 ¼ ft) tall, and has 38 strings. Pat showed me how to sit, with one leg on each side of the harp, and then how to tilt the harp and rest it on my right shoulder. I always wondered how harpists could tell which string was which note, but I noticed that although most of the strings were white, there were some red ones and some blue ones. Pat explained that the red ones are the C notes, and the blue ones are the F notes. Cool!

Pat then showed me how to place my hands and how to pluck the strings—it's harder than it looks—and I played "Hot Cross Buns," grinning the entire time. After trying a few more simple songs, I asked Pat to show me how it's *really* done. And you know what she played for me? "Early One Morning," the *Friendly Giant* theme! Loved, loved, loved it! What a wonderful afternoon.

Would I do it again?

Absolutely! Once I'm done my 60 things, I am definitely signing up for harp lessons. Can't wait!

#14 - Volunteer With the NCC

April 27th

My friend, Cathrin (my gallery visiting, belly dancing friend), asked me if I'd be interested in joining her in volunteering with the Nature Conservancy of Canada (NCC). They were looking for help to put up some Mountain Bluebird and Tree Swallow houses. I'd never heard of the NCC before, but I said, "Sure! Why not?" I'm a birder, and bluebirds are one of my favourites

We drove to Fairy Hill, which is an NCC property about 35 minutes north of Regina. It was cold and windy, but at least it wasn't raining. We met up with about 20 other people, and broke into two groups. One group would do trail clearing and the other would put up 29 birdhouses and two bat houses. Cathrin and I opted for the group that was putting up houses.

We carried the houses along the fence line, and put one up on every fifth post. The birds won't use the houses if they're too close together. They like their own space—just like people. Power drills made the job go pretty quickly.

We stopped for lunch after a couple of hours, then went to put up the bat houses.

I'd never seen bat houses up close before. They were about 60 cm wide by 66 cm tall (24 in by 26 in) and made of two sheets of brown-stained plywood with a spacer in between so that the roosting cavity was only about 2 cm (3/4 in) wide. It was open at the bottom and the back piece of plywood was longer than the front so that the bats can land on it and then climb up into the house. We screwed the two houses to the top of a long square pole, on opposite sides, then raised the pole up and screwed it to a fence post so the houses were about 3.7 m (12 ft) off the ground. The leaders told us about the bats they hoped would use these houses: Big Brown Bats, Little Brown Bats and Silver-haired Bats. Typically, these bats roost in cavities made by others, such as woodpeckers, but those cavities can often be hard to come by, so these houses would help them out. Each house can hold around 100 bats!

Would I do it again?

Yes. It was a cold, but interesting day, and I'm glad I went. Cathrin and I could both see ourselves volunteering for other projects with the Nature Conservancy of Canada. They post opportunities on their website regularly—or at least they did, before the pandemic.

#15 - Try Lawn Bowling

May 11th

I'd heard of lawn bowling but knew nothing about it, so when I discovered that the Nutana Lawn Bowling Club was having a "Come and Try It" Open House, I was in! I asked around for anyone else who wanted to join me, and Candice, Debbie (my Rush watching friend), and Marilyn (my belly dancing friend) decided to give it a go, too. Candice's sister lawn bowls and Debbie's mom did for many years, and Marilyn, like me, just likes to try new things.

We signed in and were paired with Jack and Freda, an older couple who had met through lawn bowling. As Freda put it, "I had to take it up. It's the only way I could get him to ask me out!" They were a hoot!

The bowls—don't call them balls—were about 12 cm (5 in) in diameter and weighed about 1.4 kg (3 lbs). Some were red, some were blue, and some were black. They're biased—meaning they're weighted more on one side than the other—which makes them curve rather than travel in a straight line. There's also a jack. It's white and only about 6 cm (2 ½ in) in diameter and it's not biased.

We each tried rolling the jack. Usually only the first person rolls it and then regular play begins. Most of us didn't roll it far enough to *be* in play, so Jack rolled it to get us started. We split into two teams—Debbie and Marilyn against Candice and I. Each person got two bowls. Debbie rolled one, then Candice rolled one. Debbie rolled her second one, then Candice rolled hers. Then Marilyn and I took our turns. The point is to get your bowls closest to the jack. Once all the bowls are rolled, your team gets one point for each bowl that is closer to the jack than any of the other team's bowls.

Sounds simple enough, right? There are a few things that can go wrong, though, and we managed to hit them all:

- You have to make sure you're holding the bowl with the bias on the correct side or it curves the wrong way and ends up in the neighbouring teams' game!
- You have to aim. Jack stood to show us where to aim. Bless his heart, he tried.
- You have to roll the right weight and unfortunately, unlike curling, you can't sweep it to get it to go farther.

Despite the mistakes—or maybe because of them—we had a great time!

Would I do it again?

You bet! It was a lot of fun, and is one of those sports that can be as competitive as you want it to be, which in my case, is not too much. I'm definitely signing up next year.

Update on #10

May 15th

The purple is all gone. It probably would have lasted longer if my personality wasn't type CBB—Couldn't Be Bothered. I didn't use special shampoo or wash it less, which helps keep the colour longer, but I'm okay with that. It was fun while it lasted. Now it's bleach blonde with dark blonde roots.

#16 - Go on a Hot Air Balloon Ride

May 23rd

I was really looking forward to going in a hot air balloon. I decided I better book early in the season, because it gets cancelled if the wind is over 19 km per hour (12 mph) and this *is* Saskatchewan. I did pretty good though, and only had one booking cancelled before I got to go.

We met at Kinsmen Park in Saskatoon at six in the morning and they were already filling the balloon. They fill it with cool air first and then light the heater to heat the air and lift the balloon. It's huge! Once it's inflated it's 30 m (98 ft) tall. The basket, or gondola, you ride in is 3.5 m long by 2 m wide by 1.2 m high (11 ½ ft by 6 ½ ft by 4 ft) and holds 12 people.

Lift off was amazing. Other than the occasional *whoosh* of the propane burner and the excited chatter of the passengers, it was so quiet. And smooth. And what surprised me the most—not windy. It's not windy because you're travelling *with* the wind. The only time we felt any wind was when we were moving from one layer of air to the next, because the different layers of air travel at different speeds.

We flew up to about 1100 ft (350 m) and travelled northeast

between Martensville and Warman. The view was incredible. I could even see my condo! The flight lasted about 45 minutes, and we landed just outside of Warman. We learned that balloons have the right to land anywhere, but the company tries to be a good neighbour by landing close to roads and staying away from crops.

Unlike the gentle lift off, the landing was a bit rough, which is normal. We all crouched down with our backs facing the direction we were travelling and braced ourselves, as instructed by the pilot. The gondola landed and got dragged a little ways, ending up on its side. We climbed out and then helped pack the balloon up. It's quite amazing that when packed properly it can fit into a bag that's less than 2 m (6 ½ ft) in diameter. The gondola and balloon were loaded into the recovery trailer by the chase crew, and then we were given a ride back to Kinsmen Park, where we enjoyed the traditional champagne toast to celebrate the flight.

Would I do it again?

I don't think so. I really enjoyed it, but it's not something that I feel the need to repeat.

#17 - Visit the Yukon

May 25th

My niece Amber (the head shaver) and her family live in the Yukon about half the year. They have a placer mining operation south of Dawson City. Placer—rhymes with passer—mining is the mining of stream bed deposits, which hopefully, include gold. I wanted to visit her anyway, so thought it would be a great addition to my list, and I talked my friend, Myrna, into coming with me.

We flew into Whitehorse (via Calgary and Vancouver) around 11 p.m. The sun was just *beginning* to set! Myrna's friends, George and Caroline, picked us up at the airport and dropped us off at our Airbnb accommodations.

Would I do it again?

It's too early to tell, but I imagine as long as Amber is there, there's a good possibility I'll go back.

#18 - Visit Alaska

May 27th

After a day of visiting and sightseeing in Whitehorse—they have a wonderful museum—Myrna and I took a ride on the White Pass Railway to Skagway, Alaska. First, we rode a bus for a couple of hours to Fraser, B.C., because the train only runs from Fraser on the day we wanted to go. About halfway to Fraser, we stopped at Emerald Lake. It's a beautiful blue lake that has bright green streaks around its edge and across it. We learned that the streaks are caused by light reflecting off the white deposits of marl, which is a mixture of calcium carbonate and clay. Absolutely gorgeous!

In Fraser, we transferred to the White Pass train for the 45 km (28 mi) trip to Skagway. Myrna spent most of her time outside, between the cars, taking in the amazing scenery, while I stayed inside to hear the commentary from the tour guide. It was fascinating! When I first heard that people travelling to the Yukon to strike it rich in the Gold Rush had to carry "a ton" of supplies with them, I thought it was just a way of saying "a lot" of supplies. No, they actually had to bring a ton—2000 lbs (900 kg)—of supplies with them! And load after load, they had to haul it along the White Pass Trail, which we could see remnants of from the train. The stories of the building of the railway were great, too. And the scenery? Magnificent!

We didn't have a lot of time in Skagway before we had to hop on the bus back to Whitehorse—just enough time for lunch at a seafood restaurant down by the docks and a little souvenir shopping. It was in Skagway that I got my favourite T-shirt of the trip. It has "Alaska" across the front and below it "Est. 1959"—that's the same year I was established!

Would I do it again?

There's a lot more of Alaska to see, so maybe.

#19 - Travel in a Truck Camper

May 28th

I usually tent when I'm camping, so renting a truck camper was a big deal. Myrna and I rented it from Fraser Way RV in Whitehorse and was it ever nice! A shiny new white truck with only 23 km (14 mi) on it, and a shiny new white camper to match. One of the staff went over all the features with us, and once we had all our questions answered, we were on our way.

The original plan was to drive straight up to Dawson City. However, Myrna had read an article in *Reader's Digest* about Keno City—"The Weirdest Place in the Yukon"—and really wanted to go there. Why not? It was her holiday, too. It was about an hour and a half off the Dawson City highway, but we discovered there was a campground with power in Mayo, which was a town about halfway there. (I need power because I sleep with a CPAP machine.) So the new plan was to stop in Mayo on the way to Keno, get a campsite, go to Keno, then go back and spend the night in Mayo before carrying on to Dawson City the next day. That was the plan, anyway.

We arrived at Mayo and found the campground. However, it was in the middle of renovations and they had just dug up the power cables! New plan. We would continue on to Keno—no sense turning back now—then go to Dawson from there. It would be late when we got to Dawson, but at least we didn't have to worry about driving in the dark! On we went to Keno City.

Have you ever driven into a ghost town? That's what it felt like when we reached Keno City. All that was missing was a tumbleweed rolling down the street. The *Reader's Digest* article had mentioned that there were only 20 residents, but it didn't look like any of them were home. We drove around slowly and Myrna spotted two men and a woman sitting outside one building, so she hopped out to chat. It turned out it was the Keno City Hotel, and one of the men was the owner, Leo Martel. He wondered why we had come to Keno and Myrna told him about the article—which he hadn't seen—and he laughed. The hotel was actually closed until the following week, but he opened it up and showed us around. The walls were covered with funny signs and sayings, except one wall where a beautiful quilt was hanging. Leo made it himself. The only one he's ever made, and it was stunning. He was quite a character, and had lots of stories to tell.

"Where are you spending the night?" he asked at one point.

"We were going to camp in Mayo, but they're renovating their campground, so we're driving on to Dawson from here," I explained.

"No! That's four more hours driving! You can stay here in the parking lot and go to Dawson tomorrow, if you want."

"Thanks, Leo, but I need power for the machine that I use when I sleep. Otherwise we'd happily take you up on your offer."

"I'll make you a deal," he said. "If you drive up to the top of Keno Hill to see the view, I'll hook you up with power."

"All right. Deal!"

The view was fantastic, and when we got back, Leo ran an extension cord out from the hotel and we were set for the night.

"Myrna, I have to admit, I had my doubts about this trip to Keno, but I'm really glad we did it."

"Me, too."

The truck camper was just right for the two of us. We slept like logs in "The Weirdest Place in the Yukon."

Would I do it again?

I really enjoyed the truck camper. I don't know if I would rent one again, but I *am* thinking of buying a small motorhome now.

#20 - Drink a Sourtoe Cocktail

May 30th

In Dawson City, we stayed in a campground in the middle of town, which was great because we could walk everywhere. One of the things I wanted to do for sure was join the Sourtoe Cocktail Club. It's been a Dawson City tourist tradition at the Downtown Hotel since 1973. You get a shot of Yukon Jack Whisky Liqueur into which they place a mummified human toe. Yep. It's real. The slogan is, "You can drink it fast, you can drink it slow, but your lips must touch the toe!" I downed it—the drink, not the toe—although apparently that *has* happened. Yuck—but, believe it or not, they have back-up toes. You even get a certificate, and your name and membership number entered into the log book. I'm Member #85902.

Would I do it again?

No, it's definitely a one-time thing. But I did like that liqueur, so I may have to go looking for it.

#21 - Go on a Paddlewheeler

May 31st

The *Klondike Spirit* is the only operating paddlewheeler in the Yukon. When gold was discovered near Dawson City in 1896, the Yukon River became a highway to the north and paddlewheelers regularly brought people and supplies up and down the river. Once an actual highway was constructed between Whitehorse and Dawson City in the 1950s, the age of paddlewheelers was over.

After a tour of the interior, the *Klondike Spirit* took us 5 km (3 mi) downriver to Moosehide. When the Gold Rush began, Chief Isaac moved his people, the Tr'ondëk Hwëch'in, out of Dawson to Moosehide, to preserve their way of life during the madness of gold fever. Smart man. The site is still maintained and a Gathering, that is open to everyone, is held there every summer.

Then we travelled upriver to where the Klondike and Yukon Rivers meet. The Yukon is a slower river and has a lot of silt in it, while the Klondike is faster and clearer. At the junction you can see a definite division in the water—one side is clear and the other side is muddy. Cool!

Would I do it again?

I really enjoyed it, and the *slap-slap-slapping* of the paddle-wheeler is a sound I won't forget, but it's not something I need to do again, I don't think.

#22 - Pan for Gold

June 2nd

Amber said she would take us panning for gold when we came to visit. She picked us up and took us to their camp, which is 80 km (50 mi) south of Dawson City—80 km that takes two hours to drive. The next morning we toured their operation and then gathered up pans, a shovel and a pail, and headed for the pond. Myrna had panned before, but this was a first for me. Amber filled the pail with dirt from the bank and then put a shovelful in my pan and showed me how to do it—tilting the pan, then quickly but smoothly dipping it into the water, swirling it around and repeating. Because gold is heavier than dirt, you're basically washing away the dirt, and if you've done it right, the gold stays in the bottom of the pan.

I didn't find any gold in my first pan, but I wasn't really expecting to. The next pan did yield one tiny fleck of gold, though! And some pyrite or "fool's gold," which was good so I could see the difference. Amber gave us each a little vial to put our treasure in. I was thrilled that I'd found gold! Then it got weird.

My next pan was crazy! Amber couldn't believe the amount

of gold that was in it. And not just flecks! And Myrna's was the same! We were all pretty excited. Later, the truth of our luck was uncovered. Amber had grabbed a pail that was used to haul the mats from the sluice to the washing tank, and it hadn't been rinsed out yet. So when we got to the bottom of the pail, we were actually just "finding" the gold that was in the bottom of the pail. We offered to give back the gold we had basically stolen, but Amber let us keep it.

Would I do it again?

Sure! I wouldn't want to do it for a living, but it was fun. I highly doubt I would ever strike it as rich as I inadvertently did this time, though.

Update on #17

June 5th

We flew home from the Yukon today, and I can now definitely say that I would love to return. And so would Myrna.

#23 - Ride a Ninebot

June 21st

I was a little worried about riding a Segway. I'm not the most coordinated person, and my balance can be a bit wonky sometimes. But you never know unless you try, right? My friends, Debbie (my Rush watching, lawn bowling friend) and Dave (my other Rush watching friend), met me at the Eco Glide Adventures booth in Saskatoon and Liv, our guide, suited us up with helmets, bright green safety vests and ear pieces. Then she took each of us individually and showed us how to operate our Ninebots—the brand of self-balancing personal transporter we rode, rather than Segways. It really didn't take that long to catch on. It was way easier than I was expecting. You stand on the little platform between the two wheels and hang on to the handlebars in front of you. To go forward, you just tilt slightly onto your toes. The further forward you tilt, the faster you go, but it's not an off-balancing type of tilt. To stop, you tilt slightly onto your heels. Steering is kind of by leaning—the handlebars don't turn.

Once we were all comfortable riding, we followed Liv along the paved Meewasin Trail. She would stop and tell us about different buildings and sights along the way, so it was informative as well as fun. The tour lasted about an hour, and lucky us, we got rained on—or I should say, poured on—for part of it.

Since you're basically standing in one spot the whole time, my feet were beginning to get a little sore by the end, but nothing too bad.

Lots of people smiled and shouted: "*Mall Cops*!" as we went by. Guess I'm going to have to watch that movie.

Would I do it again?

Probably not this particular tour, because "been there, done that," but Debbie and Dave have seen these machines used in other cities for tours. I wouldn't hesitate to ride one again. It would be a great way to see new places.

#24 - Volunteer at the Jazz Festival

June 22nd

I've attended the Saskatchewan Jazz Festival for a few years now, but I'd never volunteered at it. When the call for volunteers came out this time, I applied and paid the T-shirt fee, and was accepted. I missed the orientation meeting because I was "60-thing-ing" it in the Yukon, but got filled in on the details later. I would be working in the beer tent. They had a very efficient online system for signing up for shifts. By the time I got home and went on the site, there were only a couple of shifts available—an evening one and an afternoon one—so I signed up for them both. Closer to the festival date, I managed to pick up another couple of shifts.

The first shift was an evening one, and was it busy! I couldn't believe the amount of beer, wine and cider that went out of that tent. But the time flew by *because* it was so busy.

Not so much my next shift, which was an afternoon one. It didn't help that it was rainy, and a weekday afternoon. It was soooo sloooow. The nice thing about working the beer tent any time, though, is that you can hear the on-stage performers.

What I didn't know about being a volunteer (because I missed the orientation) was that if a show isn't sold out, volunteers can get in for free! *And,* volunteers get half-price liquor tickets. *And,* all the volunteers who worked at least three shifts got in free to the last show (Jann Arden), got one free drink and some snacks. What a deal!

Would I do it again?

Absolutely, but next time I would stick with evening shifts.

#25 - Visit the Tunnels of Moose Jaw

June 27th

Currently I play a borrowed valve trombone in our community jazz band. It's okay, but really, a trombone without a slide is like an ice cream sundae with no toppings—what's the fun in that? So, I started watching online for anyone selling a trombone, and found someone in Moose Jaw. That's only a two-and-a-half-hour drive away. I could do that in a day, easy! And they have the Tunnels of Moose Jaw tours, which I could do while I was there, too. A twofer! Perfect.

The tunnels are actually underground passageways in downtown Moose Jaw that were originally built between buildings in the late 1800s or early 1900s, so that steam engineers could access the boilers without having to go outside. In the late 1990s, they were transformed into a theatrical tourist attraction.

There are two tours: The Chicago Connection and Passage to Fortune. The Chicago Connection is based on Prohibition and the rumour that Al Capone used to visit Moose Jaw. The website describes the tour this way: "You're bootleggers in 1929. You come to Moose Jaw to buy booze from the Capone organization.

You've got to learn the ropes and stay out of the way of the local police chief. You start out at Miss Fanny's club and end up in a tunnel, somewhere underground. And the only one who knows the way out is Gus, one of Capone's goons." The tour guides acting was great, and it was a lot of fun.

The website describes the Passage to Fortune tour this way: "The Passage to Fortune tells the story of early Chinese immigrants to Canada. You become an Immigrant and follow in their footsteps through Burrows and Sons Laundry, in darkened tunnels under the streets and in the kitchen of Mr. Wong's cafe. Your passage to fortune is just around the corner." It was sobering. I was unaware of the horrific conditions for Chinese labourers and the challenges they had to overcome to succeed in Canada. Once again, the acting of the tour guides was great.

Someone asked me which tour I liked best, but I couldn't decide. Both were excellent. After the tours, I picked up my new trombone and drove home.

Would I do it again?

Probably not. It's one of those things that once you've done it, you've done it. But I would certainly recommend the tours to others.

#26 - Get a Personalized License Plate

July 2nd

I've never had a personalized license plate, but have often thought it would be nice—especially when I'm standing in front of a parking meter in the winter, trying to remember my plate! But what would I get? "60THNGS", what else? I ordered it a few weeks ago and it arrived today. I have to admit, it looks pretty good on my vehicle. Another way to remember this awesome year.

Would I do it again?

No need to. This will be my plate from now on.

#27 - Paddle a Dragon Boat

July 10th

When my friend, Adrienne, posted on Facebook that her dragon boat team was looking for two more members, I couldn't type fast enough to ask if I could join! I've paddled a canoe and a kayak, but never a dragon boat. She said, "Yes!"

A dragon boat is 12 m (39 ft) long, made of solid teak and weighs about 680 kg (1500 lbs). A team consists of a drummer at the front of the boat, a steersperson at the back of the boat and 20 paddlers in-between. It's a different style of paddling, but the most important thing is for everyone to paddle together.

We had three practices and a practice sprint before the actual Dragon Boat Festival. I think I got a little better each time—at least I tried to. We had an all-women team. Most of the women were younger than me, but there were a couple who were older, too. It was definitely a workout each time we were on the water.

On the big day, we had three races— and won the women's division! Okay, full disclosure—we were the only women's team this year. Although we didn't win any of our races, we held our own against the teams we raced, which were mixed teams.

An important part of the Dragon Boat Festival is the fundraising that each team does. The charities that benefit are the Children's Wish Foundation and Ronald McDonald House. Thanks to my amazing friends, I was able to raise just over $1000! Our team was the top fundraiser, raising over $10,000!

Another important part of the Festival is the Flower Toss. People buy flowers in memory of those who have died, and there's a ceremony to toss all the flowers into the river. As the top fundraising team, we got to paddle out to the middle of the river to lead the toss. I was a wreck. It's been almost five years, but Bill, I still miss you so much.

Would I do it again?

I'm glad I did it, but I don't think I'd do it again. I'm not a real competitive person. I think I'll stick to leisurely paddling my kayak.

#28 - Try Folk Dancing

July 11th

The Saskatoon International Folk Dance Club has free folk dance evenings in Kiwanis Park every Thursday during the summer.

"Cathrin—my gallery visiting, belly dancing, NCC volunteering friend—wanna try folk dancing with me?"

"Sure!" she replied immediately. Did I mention I have the best friends?

Once we found where they were in the park—we're both a little directionally-challenged—we were greeted warmly by about a dozen people, and invited to join in. They were very friendly and kind enough to pick some easier dances—out of their repertoire of 800!—for us to start with. Someone would say "how about such-and-such?" and someone else would find the music for it and we were off!

I am *not* a dancer, but it was fun! And I loved the music. Some dances I chose to just step back and watch—especially those that required you to cross one foot over the other, because I could envision a pretzel-like disaster happening. Cathrin and I were tired after an hour and left, but they continued on.

Would I do it again?

I just might. They have classes from fall to spring. It would be great exercise for both my body and my brain. I am definitely considering it.

#29 - Start Learning to Play the Trombone

July 12th

I bought a slide trombone lesson book, and have been practicing a little, but today I had my first lesson. My friend, Yvonne, plays trombone, and teaches music, and said she would help me out. I had questions. Of course. I was pretty sure I wasn't holding it right, because it just felt weird, and I was right. Yvonne straightened me out on that first thing.

"Ah, that's better. Thanks, Yvonne."

She also answered my question about slurring notes. I didn't understand the explanation in the book, but Yvonne showed me what they meant. And we glissed—that's when you slide down or up a bunch of notes, which I think is the most fun part of playing a trombone. We played together a little—I only knew a few notes—and she offered to help me out again when I got the music we'll be playing in jazz band this year. Yay!

Would I do it again?

Yes! I love playing the trombone. But I need to practice some more before I'll be ready for another lesson.

#30 - Get a Henna Tattoo

July 13th

My friend, Lianne, invited me to join her at the Farmer's Market. Great idea! I hadn't been there for a while, and wanted some fresh lettuce anyway. We wandered around and then came across a booth where a woman was doing Henna tattoos.

"Hey! I've never done *that*!"

The woman's name was Somera, and she had pages of different tattoos to choose from. I chose a hand tattoo of two leafy vines that crossed and went up the fingers. First, I had to go wash my hand though, as it had bug spray on it.

It looked like Somera was using a tube of chocolate icing. It was dark brown and quite thick. She did a really good job of the design. Plus, she fixed up the top part of my finger that I managed to smudge two seconds after she was finished. I did my best not to smear it anymore and it was dry in about half an hour. I should have asked how long I was supposed to leave the thick brown stuff on after it dried, but I didn't. So I left it on until I got home and then washed it off. Underneath, a beautiful orangey-brown design now graced my hand. Awesome!

Would I do it again?

Yes! It's beautiful *and* inexpensive, which is always nice.

#31 - Go Skinny Dipping

August 1st

When I arrived at Kimball Lake yesterday for my annual camping trip, my sister, Sheila, and her adult daughter, Brittney, were already there. I'd checked the calendar ahead of time, and knew that tomorrow night would be a new moon.

"So, who wants to go skinny dipping with me tomorrow night?" I asked hopefully. The trick with skinny dipping is you want someone to come along to watch your clothes—someone who is not going to take off with them themselves! I figured I could trust these two. Plus, it's always more fun to adventure with someone else.

"Sure! I'm in," said my niece.

"Not a chance!" said my sister. Perfect! Someone to do it with *and* someone to watch our clothes.

So the next night, the two of them came by my site at midnight, and we walked down to the beach. It was really dark when you were out of the lights of the campground. Perfect.

At Kimball Lake, the main beach, has a few lights along the path above it. Too "exposed" for skinny dipping. Even at midnight there can be someone sitting on one of the benches checking their phone, because that's where you can usually get a good signal. So we headed further down, to where the boats were moored. No lights, and no traffic.

I'm usually a "gradual-in" swimmer, but that's with a bathing suit on. Naked, I'm definitely a "run-in." The nice thing about night swimming is that since the air is cooler, the water seems warmer. Not warm, but warmer.

Brittney and I both ran in. We swam a bit, we floated a bit, we laughed a bit—but not too loudly.

"The girls sure float well," I commented as my breasts bobbed to the surface. I'm fairly well-endowed, as they say. Brittney, not so much.

"Mine just shrunk even more," she replied. Thus our nicknames for the night: Bobby and Minnie.

After about 10 minutes, we came out and dried off and dressed as quickly as we could, to avoid becoming a mosquito buffet. Then we headed back to our campsites.

Would I do it again?

I don't know. It was great to let the girls float unencumbered, but I'm 60 and midnight is pretty late to be up.

#32 - Smoke Marijuana

August 4th

Before I left for the lake, I stopped at Fire & Flower, the local pot shop. I was greeted by Abe, the budtender (a bartender for weed). I explained to him that I'd never smoked pot before but that I wanted to try it and why. He was a pleasant young man and very knowledgeable. I learned a lot.

There are two main types of pot: indica and sativa. Indica is for getting mellow—as Abe put it, think "in da couch"—while sativa is for getting high. I also learned about THC (the psychoactive component) and CBD (the non-psychoactive component). The shop has a whole wall with colour-coded labels to help you find the right type of pot with the right THC & CBD levels, depending on the experience you're looking for. Since I didn't even *know* what I was looking for, he suggested BC Sungrown Harlequin. It has a higher CBD level than THC level, so would give a more mellow experience. Sounded good to me, so I bought three pre-rolled joints.

After asking my sister and niece about skinny dipping (#31), I said, "Oh, and I also bought some pot. Wanna try it with me?"

"Sure."

"Why not?"

I love these two!

We met after supper one night, in front of a roaring campfire, and each lit up a joint. There was a little coughing at first, by me and Brittney—Sheila used to be a smoker—but we soon got the hang of it.

Have you ever licked a skunk's butt? Me neither. But I imagine it would taste very similar to smoking pot. Now I know why people get the munchies—it's to get that horrible taste out of their mouth! I was ready to eat *anything* and *everything* to get rid of it.

And mellow probably shouldn't have been what I was aiming for. After all, I'm at the lake, so I'm pretty much already at maximum mellowtitude! So it just felt like I'd had a couple of drinks—and then licked a skunk's butt.

Would I do it again?

I have no problem with anyone who does smoke pot, but I don't think it's for me. Even without the skunky taste, I'm just not wild about inhaling anything but air into my lungs. My liver and I already have an understanding—not too much, and not too often—so I think I'll stick to booze.

Update on #1 (six months)

August 15th

It's been six months since I shaved my head, and my hair is now 8.3 cm (3 ¼ in) long! I am amazed at how much it has grown. About the last 2.5 cm (1 in) of it is bleached blonde, and the rest is my regular darker blonde.

#33 - Go to Folkfest

August 15th

Folkfest is an annual celebration in Saskatoon with displays and demonstrations at different pavilions, each representing a different culture. But I hate crowds. This means that I miss out on some really good events—like Folkfest. But seeing as this is the year for doing things I've never done before—crowds be damned—I went.

I only visited six of the 17 pavilions, but for my first time, I'd say that was pretty good. I watched Scottish, Ukrainian, Greek and German dancing, listened to a Filipino children's choir and a Caribbean Steel Drum group. It was great! And I went early, so it wasn't too crowded yet, and left when it did start to get crowded.

Would I do it again?

Yes! Especially if I stick to my go-early-and-leave-when-it-gets-crowded routine, I think I could hit six new pavilions every year.

#34 - Eat Haggis

August 15th

While at Folkfest, I decided I would try that iconic Scottish dish, haggis. Of all the things I'd done so far, this was the only one I regretted. (If you're Scottish and easily offended—I'd stop reading now.) If you don't know what haggis is, it's basically ground innards and oatmeal cooked together with some spices thrown in to try and mask the disgusting taste.

I thought I had it all figured out. I would order haggis and a sticky toffee pudding. That way, if I didn't like the haggis, I could get rid of the taste with the pudding. To quote ol' Robbie: "The best laid schemes . . . Gang aft agley."

I got my scoop of haggis and my dish of pudding and sat down to enjoy some Highland dancing demonstrations while I ate. Thank goodness there was *something* to take my mind off the haggis! It was horrible! A few days before, I had asked my mom if she had ever tried haggis. She literally shuddered and said, "Yes."

"What was it like?"

"Dog food."

She was right. Now, I've never actually eaten dog food, but

haggis is exactly what I imagine it would taste like. I should add that if you like liver, you might actually like haggis. I don't. I hate liver.

So, after one bite, I knew haggis was not for me. But in honour of Scots everywhere—waste not, want not—I vowed to eat the whole damn thing. And I did. Followed by a whole bottle of water and the sticky toffee pudding—which was delicious, by the way. It got rid of the horrible haggis taste in my mouth. Or so I thought.

Haggis repeats. And repeats. In other words, for the rest of the evening, I burped haggis. It was bad enough the first time around. I began to dread the feeling of an impending burp, "Oh no! Here it comes again!"

Note to self: Next time you go to Folkfest and want to try some exotic cuisine, save it for the *last* pavilion you go to, not the first!

Would I do it again?

NO! NEIN! NEVER! And please, for those of you who are thinking, "Oh, you'd like it if you had it in Scotland," or, "if you tried it the way my Gran used to make it," or whatever—just no. There is no recipe on earth that could make that stuff taste good!

#35 - Do a Tandem Parachute Jump

August 16th

This was the scariest thing on the list: a tandem parachute jump. I wanted to do tandem rather than solo because I wanted to be attached to someone who knew what they were doing. Someone who wouldn't panic and forget what to do while falling from the sky!

This is a baaaad idea, Ennaid pronounced. I should have listened.

My friend, Rachelle, and her two kids, Rylee and Owen, joined me at the Martensville airstrip, the home of Skydive Saskatoon. While the three of them waited outside, I and the five other jumpers watched a short "no matter what happens, thou shalt not sue" video, which I thought mentioned "serious injury" and "death" way too many times. Then we signed the required forms and got weighed. You can't be over 104 kg (230 lbs) to do a tandem jump.

When I signed up, at the beginning of July, I weighed 102 kg (225 lbs). Now, normally I put on a few "ice cream" and "Chelada" pounds over the summer, but I knew I couldn't risk it this year if I wanted to do this. I was sooo good! I only had ice cream *twice* and only *one* Chelada, and that included my nine days at the lake! I amazed myself. So when it was time to weigh in, I admit, I was nervous. I stepped on the scale and . . . 102 kg (225 lbs)! Woohoo! My first thought? "If I live through this, I am definitely going for ice cream!"

Four people go up at a time—two jumpers and two jump-masters. I was in the third group. It was fun to watch the others come down with huge smiles on their faces and saying how awesome it was. When the second group went up, it was time for me to get my harness on. Mark, the guy who was doing up my harness, explained that because of my "body type" (meaning female) and how secure the harness has to be—"the girls are not going to be happy when the parachute opens." But he assured me that Jayvon, my jumpmaster, would loosen the chest strap right after the chute opened.

We headed out to the plane—a small Cessna with only the pilot seat in it. The other jumpmaster and jumper climbed in first and sat down behind the pilot with their legs outstretched and the jumper sort of between the jumpmaster's legs. While they were climbing in, Jayvon went over the jump procedure with me:

"When it's time to jump, cross your arms on your chest, lean your head back, take a deep breath, and relax. Keep your arms crossed until I tap you twice on the shoulder. Then you can stretch your arms out and fly! After the parachute opens, I'll loosen your chest strap. When we come in to land, I'll tell you when to lift your legs. And that's it! Any questions?"

Seemed pretty straightforward. Cross my arms, lean my head back, take a deep breath and relax. Got it!

We climbed into the plane—Jayvon first, then me. It took some work to get my second leg up and around the door frame.

We were really packed in. With a little scooching and leaning, we managed to get the door closed. Jayvon connected the back of my harness to the front of his, and the plane took off.

I've been in small planes before—I've flown small planes before, for that matter—so I was excited, but not scared, as we took off and climbed to altitude. Jayvon and I were going to jump from 8000 ft (2400 m) and the other guys were jumping from 11,000 (3300). It was more expensive for the extra freefall time, and 8000 seemed scary enough, thank you very much!

Unfortunately, some clouds had moved in and they were at 8000 ft. "Looks like you'll get to jump from a little higher after all," Jayvon told me. "That's okay, right?" What was I going to say? No? So, we climbed some more. Still excited, but maybe just a tad apprehensive.

You can't jump through clouds—well, physically of course you can, but you're not supposed to—so we had to circle around waiting for a hole to open up in the clouds so we could see the landing area (the jump zone). Jayvon yelled to the pilot, "I'm going to open the door early so I can get a better look." That would be the door that was inches from my leg. He opened the door and immediately my adrenaline level skyrocketed. He was leaning out to look, and I was leaning as far in the opposite direction as possible!

A hole did open up, so Jayvon got his one leg out the door, then I was to get my legs out so he could get his other leg out. It took some acrobatic moves I didn't realize I had in me, but I managed to get my legs up and around the door frame again. We were sitting in the open doorway and ready to go.

There was just one problem. Although there was nothing to hang on to with my left hand, my right hand was holding on to the door frame—and I was not letting go! My thinking brain was whispering to me, "You have to let go now, Dianne." but my survival brain was screaming at me, "ARE YOU NUTS? DO NOT LET GO! DO *NOT* LET GO!"

Jayvon managed to get my hand off the door frame but half a second later it was back on—with a death grip! It took both jumpmasters to pry my fingers off the door frame—I probably left indentations in it. Then Jayvon's instructions came back to me: Cross my ...—AND WE"RE OUT! I'm sure Jayvon figured if I ever got hold of the door frame again, I would never let go, so we went as soon as my arms were crossed.

Suddenly I was plummeting head-first towards the ground! Yes, I screamed. There is no way I could have stopped myself from screaming. It wasn't for long, but it was from every cell in my body! It was freaking terrifying!

Once we leveled out, facing the ground, Jayvon double-tapped my shoulder and I spread out my "wings." Still freaking terrifying! My voice had stopped screaming but my brain had not. People ask me how long we fell before the parachute opened. I'm not positive but I think it was about HALF A DAY! I did keep my eyes open, and my life didn't flash before them, or at least I don't think it did. I really have no recollection of thinking at all—my brain was too busy screaming to think!

Then the chute opened. Hallelujah, I'm not going to die! As Mark had predicted, the girls took a hit, but Jayvon quickly loosened the strap. Then we floated down. I watched the ground below us. It was lovely. At first.

Then my stomach began to do flips. "I wonder what happens if you puke while you're falling?" I thought. "Where does it go? Up? In my face? In Jayvon's face?"

I think Jayvon could feel me dry heaving and said, "If you're feeling nauseous, don't look at the ground. That's a bad idea.

Look up at the clouds. Aren't they lovely?"

So I looked up at the lovely clouds. But my stomach was still trying to exit my mouth.

"Do you need a bag?" Jayvon asked.

"Maybe?" I asked back.

Jayvon pulled out a bag from somewhere—obviously this must happen to others—and handed it to me. But getting a bag open while you're falling from the sky is not easy! Finally the wind caught it and it blew open. I tried to hold it up to my mouth—just in case—but it just plastered against my face. "Oh, great! If I puke, it's just going to get shmooshed all over my face! Okay. Do not puke. Do not puke." It became my mantra for the rest of the ride down.

The landing was fine. I lifted my legs. Jayvon landed and sat down and I sat down on his legs. The other people that I had watched land had all gotten up and yelled "Woohoo! I did it!" or something like that. I yelled, "Woohoo! I didn't puke!"

Rachelle, Rylee, Owen, and my friend, Diane, who arrived after I went up, all congratulated me. I hugged them like I hadn't seen them for years. And just as I had promised myself, I stopped at Dairy Queen for ice cream. Then I went home and slept for two hours. Massive adrenaline surges will do that to you.

Would I do it again?

NOT ON YOUR LIFE! I have friends who skydive for fun and love it! I have a new appreciation for just how crazy they are! Ennaid was right this time. It *was* a terrible idea. I don't regret doing it. I'm just glad it's over.

#36 - Celebrate My Birthday in the Summer

August 16th

Because I was born in the middle of February, and I live in Saskatchewan, my birthday has always involved bundling up to go anywhere and do anything. So this year, I decided to celebrate my birthday-and-a-half in August. I've never done that before! How great would it be to sit outside in the warm sunshine on my birthday. My friends, Keith and Christian, offered to throw me a summer birthday party at their place.

"You should invite 60 people!" suggested Keith. Great idea!

Of course, the one good thing about a mid-February birthday is that nobody's at the lake, or on holidays. I think about 20 people made it, though, and it was great! Everybody brought an appetizer, Keith made a killer chocolate cake, and we sat out on the back deck—until it cooled off and the wind picked up.

I had warned people that I was doing my tandem parachute jump earlier in the day, so if I didn't show up it would be because I splatted.

"Don't worry. We'll raise a glass to you, if that happens," Bette said. I tell you, friends like that are hard to come by.

But I didn't splat, and had lots of fun telling and retelling my harrowing parachute adventure. There was lots of laughter, and lots of food. What more could a birthday girl wish for?

Would I do it again?

Probably not, but everyone should celebrate a half-birthday at least once. I'm glad I did.

#37 - Drink a Martini

August 16th

The birthday party was not just a birthday party—it was also a "Martini Fest!" Keith's favourite drink is a martini and I had asked him if he would make me one sometime. That's how the idea for the Birthday Party/Martini Fest was born.

Once enough "witnesses" had arrived, Keith made the feature beverage for me. It was in a beautiful martini glass, and had three olives. I don't like olives, and Keith had offered to use something else, but I wanted the "real" martini experience, so olives it was.

I took a small sip. Was this a joke? Had he given me a glass of Pinesol by mistake?

"What do you think?" he asked eagerly.

"Ummm . . ." I hesitated.

"You have to take a bigger sip than that!"

So I did. It didn't help.

"You actually *enjoy* drinking this?" I asked him incredulously. Maybe the olives would make it taste better. If not, at least I'd be able to get the rest of it down in order to wash the olive-taste out of my mouth.

So I ate the olives. That didn't help either.

Would I do it again?

No! That stuff is horrible! My son, Troy, gave me a great description later, "It's like drinking a Christmas tree." I'll stick to rye, thank you very much.

#38 - Attend a Nudist Camp

August 18th

When my kids were little and I would be up to my knees in laundry, I used to lament, "I wish we lived in a nudist colony!" So when I was making my 60 things list, I decided to check out how far I would have to go to find one. Not as far as I thought! The Green Haven Sun Club is by Balgonie, right here in Saskatchewan. It's a trailer park, and they have trailers you can rent or spots you can reserve for your own trailer or tent. I usually tent, but wasn't sure I would be up for setting up a tent in the nude, so I phoned and booked a small trailer for a couple of days.

My mom just shook her head when I told her what my next adventure was going to be, "You're crazy."

I called when I got to the camp gates and was given the code to open them. The camp is set back from the road and surrounded by trees. One of my fears was that the first naked person I saw would be some supermodel-type, or indeed that *all* the people there would be supermodel-types. I'm more the super*size*-type. But neither of my fears was realized. The first person I saw was a middle-aged guy with a bit of a pot. Yay! I've found my people!

Lindsay, who was the manager of the camp—and also nude—greeted me and showed me to my trailer. It was an old refurbished Shasta, and only $25 a night. Perfect! She said once I got unpacked and settled in, to come on over to her trailer to do up the paperwork and then she'd take me on a tour.

I hauled my stuff—food, books, towels, but no suitcase, which felt weird—into the trailer. Then it was time to get naked! Could I really do this? Only one way to find out. I undressed, stowed my clothes away in the cupboard, and took a deep breath. I had to talk myself—and Ennaid—into it.

"You can do this." *But why?*

"Yes, it's scary, but not terrifying like jumping out of an airplane, and you did that." *And look how well that went!*

"Ready, set, go!" *Nooooo!*

I opened the trailer door and stepped out in my birthday suit.

And it was great! I was surprised at how natural it felt. I walked over to Lindsay's trailer with just my wallet and a towel—nudist etiquette: always carry a towel with you to sit on. After the paperwork and payment, Lindsay and I hopped on a golf cart for a tour.

Some people live at the camp all year, and some spend just their summers. There are families, younger people, older people—just like any other community. There weren't a lot of people there right then because it was midweek and near the end of the season. The people I met were friendly and welcoming. It was a different mindset altogether—completely non-judgmental and very freeing.

There is a sunbathing area and a playground next to an above ground pool. There's a community hall, where they hold events, and a shower house/sauna, which was right next to my trailer.

So how did I spend my time? I went in the pool one afternoon, but mostly I laid in the sun and read. I did remember to liberally apply sunscreen, especially to the parts that had never seen the sun before. Even then, I overdid it a bit and burned a few of those virgin areas. And I chatted with other people. It was not uncomfortable at all! In fact, I think I was less shy meeting new people in the nude than I usually am meeting people fully-dressed! Very surprising. It definitely goes to show—you never know until you try.

Would I do it again?

Absolutely! In fact, before I left, I booked the trailer for a few days next summer.

#39 - Attend a Sing-along Movie

August 31st

I've seen ads for sing-along movies before, but I'd never been to one. I would have preferred to go to *The Sound of Music*, but that's not what was playing. *Grease* was, with John Travolta and Olivia Newton-John. I couldn't remember if I saw the movie when it first came out in 1978, but I definitely remember the hits from it. I even have the soundtrack on vinyl.

I called up my friend, Debbie (my Rush watching, lawn bowling, Ninebot riding friend), and she agreed to join me. We arrived early to get good seats. It wasn't a full house, but there were a lot of people. Some old, some young, some dressed up in costume. A crowd that was ready to have some fun.

When you entered the theatre, you got a little paper bag of props: a balloon, a party horn, and a big white paper napkin. Some people used the props, but we didn't. I just wanted to sing along.

Before the show started, an energetic young woman led us through a little warm up, showed us what the props were for, and tried to teach us the Hand Jive. I could do it if it was really slow, but it fell apart when I tried it faster. I was just happy I didn't end up slapping myself in the face! We were also encouraged to make sound effects—cheering, booing, crying, hissing—at the appropriate times.

Then the movie started. It was fun to sing along to the songs I remembered from my early 20s, despite the cringe-worthy lyrics—"Tell me more, tell me more, did she put up a fight?"—and despite how cheesy the movie was.

Would I do it again?

If it was a different movie, sure! "The hills are alive . . ."

Update on #11

September 4th

Have you ever wondered how long it takes for your nails to completely replace themselves? I have. So when I got my manicure I decided to leave the shellac on and see how long it would take to grow out. It took five months. I clipped off the last little red sliver on my thumbs today. Now you know.

#40 - Try Paddleboarding

September 8th

Paddleboarding is the new craze, so I thought I would give it a try, knowing full well that I have the balance of a drunken giraffe. Good thing I'm not afraid to get wet.

My friend, Dave (my Rush watching, Ninebot riding friend), offered to let me try his paddleboard, and said he would teach me what to do. Yay! We met at a pond in the Saskatoon neighbourhood of Briarwood. I was amazed to find out that his paddleboard was actually an inflatable one. I guess I thought if it was inflatable it would be softer, more like an air mattress. But it's inflated to 15 psi, so it's solid. Dave showed me, on land, how to get on the board—on hands and knees, feet shoulder width apart, then place one foot on each side of the centre handle, place the paddle across the board in front of you, and stand up. Sounded simple enough.

Then we moved onto the water. Thankfully, Dave held the board still for me, while I clambered on, and then, miracle-of-miracles, stood up! He reminded me to keep my knees slightly bent, and then he let go. Immediately I could see ripples forming around the board as I worked to keep my balance.

"Okay, you've got it. Now, do you want to try again without me holding on?" Dave offered.

"Are you kidding?" I exclaimed. "I'm up! Why mess with a good thing?"

Then I slowly and carefully paddled out to the middle of the pond. I slowly and carefully turned around, and then I slowly and carefully paddled back to shore. Without falling in! Amazing! Must have been the great teacher I had.

Would I do it again?

Probably not. It was okay. I didn't hate it. But I prefer my kayak.

#41 - Compose a Choir Piece

September 10th

I've been a member of our church choir, the Contemporary Singers, for many years. I decided to challenge myself to try and write a choir piece. Big challenge since I'm not strong on music theory. But I have a pretty good ear.

So, what to write? The United Church has a statement of faith called "A New Creed." It's not so new anymore, but I have always loved it. It starts and ends with "We are not alone." Powerful and comforting at the same time. I'd checked around and found some musical adaptations of it, but none that I really liked. So why not try writing one of my own? Plus, then I only had to come up with the music, not the music *and* the words.

I worked away on it for about a month, using a great free computer program called MuseScore. I wrote it for three parts: Soprano, Alto and Baritone. Then I asked our fantastic pianist, Erin (my axe throwing, belly dancing friend), if she would write an accompaniment for it. Thankfully, she said yes, because I know even less about writing accompaniments than I do about writing choir parts.

When it was done, I asked our director, Keith (my party

hosting, martini making friend), if he would mind if we tried it out. Not only did he enthusiastically agree, but he convinced me to conduct it as well! And he set a date for when we would sing it at a service.

I decided that the first practice would be the official date of accomplishing this goal. The practice wasn't great, honestly. I'd directed a choir before, but not one this big. And I was so overwhelmed that we were singing something *I* wrote that I was basically useless. Thank goodness for Erin, who got us through it. I'm sure I'll get it together for the next practice.

Would I do it again?

I would love to take a class or classes on composing music. So yes, if I learn more about it, I'd love to do more.

Update on #6 (six months)

September 11th

I've been learning German on Duolingo for six months now, and I'm still enjoying it. German is such an economical language. You don't need a brand-new word for everything, you just put two old ones together! For instance, Zeug *means "stuff." So then "Airplane" is* Flugzeug *(flight stuff), "Vehicle" is* Fahrzeug *(drive stuff), and "Toy" is* Spielzeug *(game stuff). How cool is that!*

#42 - Compose a Handbell Piece

September 24th

I've been playing handbells for about eight years, and currently play in two different groups: our church group and a more advanced group. So why not try arranging a piece for handbells? I decided to use "What a Friend We Have Jesus" because I like the tune, and it's in the public domain. I used MuseScore again and wrote it for a 3-octave group, which our church group is.

Well, we tried it tonight, so I can officially claim I did it, but it didn't go very well. I forgot to list what bells were needed, and it was probably a little too difficult. Oh well, can't win 'em all. It was still fun to try.

Would I do it again?

Again, maybe if I took some composition classes. We'll see.

#43 - Visit the (2nd) Biggest Tree in Saskatchewan

October 10th

Visiting the largest tree (as in the widest trunk) in Saskatchewan was on my list from the beginning. I called up Cathrin (my gallery visiting, belly dancing, NCC volunteering, folk dancing friend) and Lianne (my henna tattoo friend) to see if they wanted to go adventuring with me.

"Sure!" they both said. So we set a date to go, and wouldn't you know it—as soon as we made our plans to go see the largest tree in Saskatchewan, it got dethroned! Apparently there's a tree in someone's yard in Saskatoon that is now the largest. Hmmmph! What's the fun in going to see a tree in somebody's yard? So we went to see the *second* largest tree in Saskatchewan instead. Never done it before. It still counts.

I knew the general directions—about 15 km (9 mi) past the Petrofka bridge, turn right onto Tree Road. There's a blue sign that says Doukhobor caves. We travelled a ways down that road and were so busy chatting we would have missed the next turn, but thankfully, eagle-eyed Lianne saw the sign to turn right. From there it was trial and error. We came to an intersection but didn't know if we were supposed to go straight or turn left. We went straight for a little bit, then decided the tree was probably closer to the river so backtracked and took the other road. It took us down into a gorgeous river valley. We all agreed that even if we didn't find the tree, the view was worth the drive. The road became more like a path, but we continued on.

"If we come to the river or this becomes a cow path before we find the tree, we'll turn around," we agreed. Then we drove around the next turn and there it was! It was definitely impressive. It's called the Popoff tree, "named after Samuel J. Popoff who leased the crown land on which the tree is located." That's what the sign next to the tree said. It also said that the tree was a Plains Cottonwood/Poplar cross and was over 160 years old! That's older than Canada! It's only 21 m (69 ft) high now because the top of the tree was sheared off by lightning, but its circumference is about 5 m (16 ft). Doing a little math (because I'm nerdy that way), I figured the diameter of the tree was about1.6 m (5 1/4 ft). Some of the branches that have fallen off looked like trunks themselves. Amazing!

Would I do it again?

Strangely, yes! It's a beautiful drive, and I think I'm even more partial to it now that it's only the second biggest tree in the province.

#44 - Visit the Crooked Trees

October 10th

After visiting the Popoff tree (#43), we continued on to visit the Crooked Trees. There was no sign this time to tell us where to turn off the highway, but Google Maps did not let us down. There *was* a sign showing where to turn off the grid road. We were chatting as usual, and almost drove right by the Crooked Trees, or "Crooked Bush" as the sign says. We pulled into the little parking lot and went to check them out. It's not a big area, but it's interesting. The trees are Aspens and on one side of the parking lot, they are straight and normal-looking. But on the other side, the trees are really warped-looking. Nothing is straight—the trunks bend and turn in all sorts of weird and wonderful ways. There's a wooden walkway that takes you through the Crooked Trees. I was so engrossed in looking at the trees that I didn't notice a branch that crossed the wooden walkway at about head height. Well, actually, at *exactly* head height. Ouch!

Would I do it again?

Probably not. It was cool to see, but I think once is enough.

#45 - Volunteer at Ronald McDonald House

October 31st

The dragon boat team that I was part of in the summer (#27) asked if anyone would be interested in volunteering at Ronald McDonald House. Count me in! Not only because I had never done it before, but also because I think it's an awesome facility. Any family from outside of Saskatoon who has a child receiving medical attention in the city, can stay at Ronald McDonald House for $10 a night, and if that is a barrier, it can be waived. The house can accommodate 34 families and is only a short walk from the Jim Pattison Children's Hospital. The program we volunteered for was "Home for Dinner." Groups can sign up to supply and cook a meal for the families. We chose to do it on Halloween.

Our team leaders, Jolene and Adrienne, decided we'd make Tacos in a Bag. A great casual meal for Halloween, I thought. The food is served from 6:00 to 7:00, so we were told to come at 5:00 to get everything ready. We were also encouraged to dress up, so I wore the rainbow wool wig I made when I was bald. Then we were each given a different coloured T-shirt with a giant M on it—we were M&Ms!

Adrienne and Jolene had already fried up all the hamburger meat by the time the rest of us arrived. So we just had to pour the hamburger into slow cookers, cut open the taco chip bags, and pour the lettuce, cheese, salsa and sour cream into bowls. Then just before 6:00 we put out the food and the families started to arrive. The organizers had told us to prepare for about 80 people. They have large commercial fridges, and leftovers are always appreciated, since some families are still at the hospital at supper time.

Some of the kids were dressed in costumes and were going to go trick-or-treating in the neighbourhood after supper. How wonderful that these families are able to have some fun even while going through what must be some very difficult times. One little girl who was dressed up as a fairy was fascinated by my wig and wanted to touch it, so I squatted down and let her feel it. What a sweetheart!

We stayed to clean up after supper. With eight of us, it didn't take long. This was definitely the most rewarding thing I had done so far.

Would I do it again?

Absolutely! I told the other women that although I wasn't going to be paddling again, I would definitely help out if they planned to do another "Home for Dinner" at Ronald McDonald House.

#46 - Attend a Pow Wow

November 1st

"The Spirit of Our Nations Cultural Celebration and Pow Wow" is an annual event put on by the Federation of Sovereign Indigenous Nations (FSIN). It's the largest pow wow in the province, with competitors coming from all across North America and is held at Sasktel Centre, which is the biggest sporting facility in Saskatoon. Standing in line to get in, it was fun to see people hugging and shaking hands with others they obviously hadn't seen in a while, maybe since the last pow wow. Some were dancers—either dressed in their regalia or carrying it—some were drummers carrying gear, and some were spectators, like me.

As I neared the table where you paid to get in, I noticed a sign that said "We respect our elders. Free admission for those 60+." Nice! I was a bit tentative when I told the woman at the table, "I'm 60." but she just gave me a big smile and said, "Then go on in! And enjoy!" So welcoming.

After wandering around the mezzanine to check out the various vendors, I chose a seat that gave me a good view of the event floor. The announcers sat at a table on a raised platform at one end. Around the edge of the event floor there were drums—about 15 of them, I think. Each was from a different drumming group. The drums are large and lie horizontally rather than being held vertically like a bass drum, and are played by a group of drummers that sit around them.

Prior to the Grand Entry, which is the official beginning of the pow wow, each drumming group did one short song. Like any music that is unfamiliar, it took me a while to get used to it, but I soon began to appreciate the skill of the drummers, in singing as well as drumming. The beat is so important and begins to feel like the heartbeat of the whole gathering. My favourite drum group was the Cree Canaries. They are a father (Mario Fiddler) and his three young sons. The boys were the youngest drummers there, but no less respected.

The Grand Entry began with the dignitaries. After all the dignitaries entered and were introduced, the veterans entered and were introduced as well. This was not rushed. It was important. Each vet was introduced with where they were from and where they had served. Widows were also introduced and honoured, and their husband's name and where they had served were announced. It was so respectful.

All the chiefs that were in attendance also entered and were introduced. Again, this was not rushed. It was too important for that.

Then the dancers began to enter, in their categories based on the type of dance and their age. One thing I noticed is that there was a pair of elders sitting by the entrance to the event floor, and each and every dancer stopped to pay their respect to them—even the smallest children. It was beautiful to see.

More and more dancers entered until there were over 600 people on the event floor. With all the colourful regalia, it was an amazing sight.

After the Grand Entry, but before the competitions began, there was an Intertribal dance led by the Whip Man. It was explained that all dancers should participate and if the Whip Man called you from the stands to dance you had to go. Everyone danced in a clockwise direction around the event floor except for the Whip Man who danced counter-clockwise.

After the Intertribal dance, the competitions began. Each group would do two dances, with a different group drumming for each dance. There were judges around the event floor, watching the dancers. After the dances, the judges conferred, then the dancers were called over to the side and the winners were chosen, but that wasn't the focus. The winners weren't even announced over the speakers. It seemed less about winning and more about celebrating their culture. I really liked that about it.

I didn't stay for the entire event. I left after about four hours. But I left impressed. There was such a feeling of pride and community and respect. I loved it.

Would I do it again?

Yes! Maybe to a smaller one next time, but I thought it was fascinating.

Update on #41

November 3rd

At church this morning the Contemporary Singers sang We Are Not Alone, the piece I wrote. I was a bit nervous, but I think it went really well. A great experience, but in the future, I think I'll stick to creating. Conducting is not my forté, nor my interest. There's just too much going on all at once!

#47 - Eat Smoked Cheese

November 6th

Sometimes it's the little things.

We have a terrific local butcher shop here in Martensville—the Smoke Haus. I often stop there after coming home from visiting my mom and buy a small package of Honey Garlic Beer Sticks—my favourite. Today, there was a line-up at the cash register, and as I was waiting in front of the display case, I noticed they had small blocks of Smoked Cheddar Cheese.

"Hmmm. I've never had that before. Might be good. Can't possibly be as bad as haggis!" It didn't take long to talk myself into buying a block.

I'd eaten half the beer sticks by the time I got home, but figured I'd save the other two in case I didn't like the smoked cheese. I opened the package and this wonderful smoky aroma escaped. I cut a small piece and put it in my mouth. Mmm-mmmm! It was so delicious! The best way I can think of to describe it is that it was like having a campfire in your mouth. Not because it was hot like a fire, but because it evoked summer and camping and sitting around a fire in the evening. So good!

Would I do it again?

Absolutely! I had to ration myself to one piece a day, or it would have been gone in no time. And not to sound old or anything but at my age—or really at any age—a whole block of cheese in one day is probably not the best gift you can give your innards.

#48 - Attend a Buddhist Meditation Class

November 17th

Most people aren't aware that there is a Buddhist monastery just outside of Saskatoon. I wasn't either until I saw it mentioned in the local paper. The monastery holds a free Buddhist Meditation class every Sunday afternoon.

Before I went, I checked out their very informative website and learned that the monastery and meditation centre opened in 2015. On their website they also have an excellent "What to Expect" page. I learned that there is no dress code, other than to dress modestly, but you have to remove your shoes when you enter. You can sit on the floor, on a cushion, or on a stool or chair. I also learned that the monks, who wear robes and shave their heads, don't shake hands, but you can greet them with a smile or by placing your palms together in front of your chest, or by bowing.

Google Maps directed me to the monastery—a beautiful log house about ten minutes out of Saskatoon. I took off my coat and boots when I entered and found a little stool to sit on in the third row of mats. There were four rows altogether. The mats are set up in front of a rectangular table that holds a statue of Buddha, as well as flowers and candles.

There are also two smaller round tables, one on each side of the rectangular one. One holds a ceramic pot with a Bodhi Tree in it. It was explained that 2600 years ago the prince Siddhartha, while sitting under a tree, attained enlightenment and became Buddha. A branch from that tree, called the Bodhi tree, was brought to Anuradhpura City in Sri Lanka 236 years after Buddha died, and remains there today. The Bodhi tree at this monastery is a clone of the one in Anuradhpura.

The other round table holds a small Relic Casket, which contains sacred items such as Bodhi leaves.

The mats on the floor each had a booklet with the words to the chants in it, both in English and in Pali, which is the ancient language of Buddhism. The monk that led the meditation sat on the floor in front and to the right of the tables. First he paid homage to Buddha in Pali and then in English. The only Pali word I remember is *Sadhu*, which means "excellent." Then came the "Going for refuge to the Triple Gem" chant—the Triple Gem being Buddha, the Dhamma (the teachings of Buddha), and Sangha (the enlightened ones). Both of these chants we could say along with the monk.

Next we observed the five precepts, by repeating them after the monk. Basically they are to abstain from killing, stealing, sexual misconduct, lying, and intoxicating substances.

Then the monk read a lesson about Karma. Buddhists believe that the Karma you collected in your previous lives affects your current life, and the Karma you collect in your current life affects the future of this life and your next lives. It was an interesting point of view—not one that I share, but that's okay.

We ended by chanting the discourse on loving-kindness.

I had read about it on the website: "This meditation trains our mind to have thoughts for the welfare of all living beings whether they are near or far away, friendly or unfriendly, large or small, visible or invisible. By training ourselves with this kind of meditation we can slowly give up our habits of anger and resentment. It is also very useful for calming and focusing your mind." It goes like this:

May I be free from anger.
May I be free from ill will.
May I be free from jealousy.
May I be free from mental suffering.
May I be free from physical suffering.
May I live in peace. May I live happily.

We chanted the whole thing quite a few times—the first time using *May I*, then *May all beings in this place*, then *May all beings in this area*, and continuing to expand it each time to city, province, country, and so on, finishing with *May all beings*. I found the rhythm of the words very calming.

Would I do it again?

It was an interesting 90 minutes and I'm glad I went, but I don't think I would go again.

#49 - Try Tenpin Bowling

November 22nd

Fivepin bowling is a Canadian game. I learned to bowl fivepin in Meadow Lake when I was a kid, and Bill and I belonged to a fivepin league for a few years in Saskatoon, but it dawned on me last week that I'd never bowled tenpin. The differences are the number of pins, of course, but also the size of the balls, and the scoring. In tenpin, the pins are worth one point each, while in fivepin, the pins are worth either two, three or five points, depending on their position. The balls are larger in tenpin, and have three finger holes.

I phoned Eastview Bowl and booked a lane, then put out the call for friends to join me. Betty Lou (my axe throwing friend), Cathrin (my gallery visiting, belly dancing, NCC volunteering, folk dancing, tree viewing friend) and Chris, Keith (my party hosting, martini making, choir director friend) and Christian (my other party hosting friend), and Scott were in.

I thought bowling was a dying sport, so I was surprised to find the parking lot full on a non-league night. We all checked in and paid and got our shoes—just as stylish as I remembered. What I didn't remember was the noise! Music was blasting away, and the place was packed, so it was really loud. Who knew bowling was so popular? If you wanted to have a conversation you basically had to yell at each other.

"I love this song!" Scott yelled to me at one point.

"Really? I can't even hear what song it is!" I yelled back.

We did have fun, though. We bowled for an hour, which was enough time to play a couple of games. I even got a few strikes!

Would I do it again?

Not to sound like an old lady again, but no—it was too dang loud in there!

#50 - Tour a Mosque

November 24th

The largest mosque in Saskatchewan is in Saskatoon and once a month they have an open house. I mentioned it to the members of my church choir and Barb (my axe throwing, belly dancing friend), Brenda, Erin (my axe throwing, belly dancing, choir accompanist friend) and Murray (another axe throwing friend), and Ken and Maryann decided to come, too.

Normally the open house starts at noon, but I phoned the mosque and explained that on the day we wanted to come we were singing at the 9:30 service and would be done at 10:30. Would it be possible to come at 11:00? Rashid, the tour guide for that day, said, "No problem."

The Baitur Rahmat Mosque was built in 2016 on the outskirts of Saskatoon. It's a large cream-coloured building with one large dome, a smaller dome and a minaret. Rashid met us at the door, and told us he would take us on a tour of the building, show us a display about the Ahmadiyya Muslims, and then we were invited to stay for refreshments. He was so welcoming. He also explained that men and women don't shake hands with each other.

The first thing he pointed out was the digital clock on the wall. Muslims pray five times a day—at dawn, noon, midafternoon, sunset and evening. Since the times are based on the rising and setting of the sun, the clock shows what the prayer times for that day are.

In the hallway are pictures of their leaders, the past and current Caliphs of Ahmadiyya Muslims. We stopped in the library and Rashid explained that the Ahmadis were originally from Pakistan, but their religion was outlawed, so many of them immigrated to Canada. They are a Muslim sect that was founded in 1889, and who believe that the Messiah returned in the person of Mirza Ghulam Ahmad. They believe that Jesus and Buddha and other religious persons were all prophets and so accord them respect.

Besides the Qur'an and the sayings of Prophet Muhammad, the Ahmadis also study the writings of and about Mirza Ghulam Ahmad. He wrote over 90 books.

We were also shown the gymnasium. They hold community sports here, open to all. Then we went to the hall, where they had the displays set up and an elder told us a bit more about their beliefs and practices and we had a chance to ask questions. It was very interesting. They stressed that Muslims are a peaceful people, as the Qur'an instructs them to be.

Then we went to the large prayer hall. We removed our shoes before entering. It has lovely plush carpeting, and is under the large dome. Muslims pray wherever they are, but on Fridays, at noon, many people come to pray at the mosque. Men and women pray in separate areas. This large prayer hall is where the men pray.

Then we had refreshments, back in the hall with the displays. As we were leaving, I thanked Rashid, and because I wasn't thinking, I stuck out my hand to shake his. But I quickly realized what I was doing—partly by the hesitant look on his face—and pulled my hand back. Eloquent as ever, I said "Oops. Sorry." He just smiled and thanked us for coming and invited us to come back any time.

Would I do it again?

It was interesting and I was glad I went, but I probably wouldn't repeat the tour.

#51 - Visit the Canadian Light Source Synchrotron

December 9th

The Canadian Light Source synchrotron is a research facility on the University of Saskatchewan campus in Saskatoon, and the only one of its kind in Canada. They offer free public tours on Mondays, Wednesdays and Fridays.

The front entrance isn't really well-marked, but I eventually found it. I was met by the tour guide, who showed me where I could hang up my coat, had me sign in and gave me a visitor badge on a lanyard to wear. I was a little early, so I sat in the lobby and waited for the other six people who had signed up for the tour.

Once everyone arrived, our guide opened the security door with his key card and we followed him through the door and up a staircase to the mezzanine. It runs above and around the outside of the synchrotron itself. Along the walls of the mezzanine there were posters that helped explain how it works, who uses it, and some of the things it has been used for.

Here's what I learned:

- The synchrotron opened in 2004 and cost $173.5 million to build.
- A beam of electrons is shot into the linear accelerator where microwaves increase the energy of the electrons over 1000 times, and increases their speed to almost the speed of light! Then they get transferred into a booster ring and a radio frequency cavity to increase their energy even more, and then into a storage ring. Magnets in the storage ring bend the electron beam, releasing an intense beam of light which is directed down 23 different beam lines where researchers use the light to investigate their samples at the molecular level. It's sort of like really really really high-resolution x-rays.
- Researchers from all over the world book time on the synchrotron, which is available up to 5000 hours per year. All 23 beam lines can be used simultaneously, so that's 115,000 hours of research time per year!
- All kinds of research projects are done there—medical, agricultural, mining, environmental, archeological, food science—you name it. A couple of projects that I remembered were the production of medical isotopes, and reducing the cooking time of lentils.
- They even have a program where school kids can come up with a project and use the synchrotron to investigate it.

Would I do it again?

Actually, I would. It was really interesting and a lot to take in at one time, so I wouldn't mind going through it again.

#52 - Get a Reflexology Treatment

December 20th

I've done Reiki and acupuncture but never reflexology, so I thought it was time to give it a try.

I went on our local "Ask and Rant Away" page on Facebook and asked for recommendations for reflexologists, preferably right here in Martensville. Kathy Neufeld's name came up, so I called her and booked a one-hour appointment. She works out of her home.

As soon as I saw her, Kathy looked familiar. Turns out she had been an Educational Assistant in my sons' school. I caught her up on where my boys were now. Small world.

We went into her treatment room and she gave me a detailed form to fill out regarding any medical conditions in my past or present, and any problems I was currently having. Then we went over it together, and she asked some more questions.

I explained that I didn't have any current problems, but just wanted to try reflexology, and told her about my 60 Things project. I took off my socks and sat in a reclining zero-gravity chair. Kathy gave me a warm blanket to cover up with and explained to me the idea behind reflexology—that there are paths of energy that run through your body. These paths have end points in your feet, and so by massaging these areas you can improve the flow of energy, which therefore improves your health. She had a chart on the wall that showed the different areas of each foot and what parts of the body they corresponded to.

I thought I might be uncomfortable with somebody rubbing my feet—I wasn't wild about the pedicure I got once—but it was fine. She massaged each toe, and everything was good until she got to my big toe.

"Ooh, that's a little sore," I said.

"Is your neck bothering you?" she asked. "You didn't mention it on your questionnaire."

"Well, a little, but just the usual stiffness from turtling in the cold and too much time on the computer," I replied. I was amazed that pain in my big toe indicated to her that my neck was sore. Very cool.

I can't say I noticed any difference in my neck afterwards, but my feet felt great, and I felt very relaxed.

Would I do it again?

Sure! It would be interesting to learn more about it, so maybe I'll even sign up for a class at some point.

#53 - Drive a Snowmobile

December 25th

Since my husband's death a few years ago, I go to my sister Sheila's (my clothes watching, pot smoking friend) for Christmas supper. My brother-in-law Don and my nephew Austin both have snowmobiles, so this year, I asked Austin if he could bring his machine over to his parents' place and if I could drive it. I know a lot of people who love to go "sledding" in the winter, so I thought it was time I checked it out.

Not only did Austin bring his snowmobile over, he and Don went out earlier and made a trail around the schoolyard behind Sheila and Don's place. So after opening presents, and while it was still light out, Austin and I went for a ride. First thing I found out—those helmets are heavy! Mine had a face shield on it, which I had to crack open a bit because I kept fogging it up—menopausal women throw off heat at the worst times!

Austin showed me the controls—throttle is on the right handlebar, brake is on the left.

"Okay, Austin. I'll follow you. Just don't go too fast." Then we started them up. Wow, it was even louder than I was expecting!

So for the next 15 minutes or so, we drove around the schoolyard. Slowly at first, and then a little faster as I got more comfortable. No catastrophes. I didn't run into anything. I didn't fall off. I didn't stall out. It was all good.

We turned back into the yard and shut off the machines. Aah, blessed silence!

Would I do it again?

No. Sorry, but I don't get the attraction. It's noisy and you smell like gas when you're done. I'd much rather go for a walk or even a snowshoe.

#54 - Try Downhill Skiing

January 11th

I tried cross-country skiing when I was in school as part of Phys. Ed., but I'd never done downhill before. I'm leaving for Hawaii in a week, so I debated whether this was a good idea or not, but I decided if I took a lesson and stuck to the bunny hill, I should be okay.

As usual I asked if anyone wanted to join me, explaining that I'd never skied downhill before. Lots of people thought I was crazy, or they had injury-laden flashbacks they felt the need to share, but my friend, Karen (my belly dancing friend), said she was game. She had downhill skied before but not for a lot of years, so she was happy to take a lesson with me.

Karen picked me up and we drove to Table Mountain, just outside of North Battleford. We live on the prairies, so we don't actually have any mountains. But because we live on the prairies, we're used to making do—so we ski down the sides of valleys instead.

We rented skis, boots, and poles, and I rented a helmet as well. Walking around in the boots, I felt like Frankenstein's monster. Whoever first filmed that movie must have been a skier.

After one last bathroom stop, we carried our skis and went to wait at the designated "Lesson Bench" for Victor, our instructor. He was a young man in his thirties. Before heading to the bunny hill, he showed us the two basic moves to go and to stop—or as my son, Greg, told me: "French fries and Pizza." To go, you want your skis parallel—like french fries. To slow down or stop, you want to point the tips toward each other to form a V—like a slice of pizza.

"And if you ever feel out of control, don't panic. Just fall down," was Victor's final piece of advice before we went over to the hill. Walking in skis is not as effortless as they make it look on TV—at least not when I do it. But we made it to the hill eventually.

Then came the trickiest manoeuvre of the day—getting on the "Magic Carpet." It's a continuously running conveyor belt that you ride to the top of the hill. Sounds simple, right? It wasn't! Oh, riding it was fine, but getting on it was a challenge.

"Bend your knees, and lean forward a bit. Keep your poles up, under your arms. Move forward until the belt takes your skis." Victor explained it very well.

Karen went first, and did fine.

My turn. Okay, knees bent, lean forward, move forward . . . Aaaaah! My skis took off, while my upper body tried to stay behind. I didn't fall, but it was close.

"That's okay. I'll be ready next time," I thought, as I was carried up the hill.

Getting off, you again bend your knees and lean forward. There's a little decline at the top so you ski off the carpet and then turn to your right or left to get out of the way of whoever is coming behind you. I did okay getting off. Karen had a harder time getting comfortable with getting off.

Victor showed us to go diagonally down the hill so that the descent wasn't so steep. We practiced our French Fries and Pizzas going across the hill. Then we would stop and turn our skis to go back across the other way, repeating that until we got to the bottom. Time to tackle the "Magic Carpet" again!

This time I would be ready for when it grabbed my skis. Poles up, knees bent, lean forward. Not close enough. Inch forward. Inch forward. Inch—and gone! Aaaah! Not ready. Not quite as bad as the first time, but it still caught me off guard, and I had to fling my upper body forward to keep from falling over backwards. For the rest of the afternoon, every time I attempted to get on, I thought I would be ready for the lurch. Every time I was wrong. I renamed it the "Spastic Carpet."

The next thing we learned was how to turn—you shift your weight onto the ski on the inside of the turn and take your weight off the other ski. For some reason I could turn right a lot easier than I could turn left. But the important thing was that I didn't fall and break anything.

Once the one-hour lesson was over, Victor said good-bye, and we did a couple of more runs on the bunny hill before we headed back to the chalet for a pee break.

Victor had explained that the Tom Shaw run was like the bunny hill as far as the grade, but just longer, if we wanted to take the chairlift up and try it. Normally, I would have said, "Why not give it a try, since we're here?" But I was going to Hawaii next week. So far, I hadn't fallen, despite the Spastic Carpet's best efforts, so I figured—why tempt fate?

I think Karen and I were both on the same page, but neither was sure how to broach it. After our little break, I jumped in with, "You know, whenever you're ready to go, just say so. We don't have to stay all day."

"Okay."

Hmmm. Too subtle. I tried again. "Even if you want to call it quits now, I'd be okay with that. I came, I saw, I didn't fall. I'm good."

"That works for me," Karen agreed. Yay!

We returned our equipment and drove home.

Would I do it again?

I'm not a huge fan of being outside in the winter, so probably not. And if it means not having to get on that stupid conveyor belt again, I would be happy never to ski again.

#55 - Visit Hawaii

January 16th

Saskatchewan was in the second week of a cold snap with temperatures in the -25° to -40°C (-13° to -40°F) range, so I was really looking forward to going somewhere warm. The taxi picked me up at 5:00 a.m. and took me to the airport for my 7:30 flight to Hawaii.

It was a long day. I flew from Saskatoon to Edmonton, then had to wait eight hours before my flight to Vancouver, and another two-hour wait until my six-and-a-half-hour flight to Honolulu. But worth it.

My friend, Jo, had invited me to come visit her at her condo in Waikiki. It was a beautiful place. Two bedrooms, a big living room, a kitchen and dining room. There were two balconies—one off the living room and one off the dining room—that both faced the ocean, and you could see the marina to the right.

Jo took me on a tour of the complex and I did my best to try and learn my way around. The good thing is I'm not afraid of getting lost—because I do it so frequently.

The weather was amazing. Not too hot, and the same every

day. I got up early each morning, had my breakfast on the balcony, and then took my camera and went birding. I had been hoping to go on a birding tour while I was there, but it didn't work out, so I decided just to wander around on my own and see what birds I could find. (I ended up with 19 new birds for my life list during the trip, which I thought was pretty good.)

We ate at a lot of great restaurants. The Liliha Bakery was memorable. Jo's brother and sister-in-law had eaten there with Jo previously, and Nairn had ordered the fried chicken. You could order one, two, or three pieces, and he's a big guy so he ordered three pieces. Jo told me he couldn't finish it. So I only ordered two pieces. Well, I don't know what they feed their chickens in Hawaii, but I got two of the biggest pieces of breast meat I had ever seen! They were enormous! I cannot imagine the size of the chicken they must have come from. Let's just say I wouldn't want to meet it in a dark alley with bird seed in my pocket. I managed to eat one piece and we had sandwiches for two days afterwards with the other piece.

During the week, we also went to a luau at Paradise Cove, a 45-minute bus ride from the condo. Along the way I learned from the guide that all Hawaiian words end in a vowel. I hadn't noticed that. I also saw cactuses—something I never would have guessed I'd see in Hawaii.

Paradise Cove was a beautiful setting, right on the oceanfront. They had musicians playing and demonstrations of native Hawaiian skills, such as throwing out fishing nets, shimmying up a palm tree, and of course, hula dancing. Then we were all invited to an outdoor amphitheater to see some traditional Hawaiian dances and for the imu ceremony. The imu is the pit that the pig is cooked in. The ceremony involved removing the layers of cloth and leaves and then lifting the roast pig out of the pit. It smelled so good! Then it's taken to the kitchen where the meat is shredded for the buffet.

The food was plentiful and delicious. I took a little of what I thought was some kind of chopped tomato salad, but found out later it was poke, which is diced raw fish. No wonder it didn't taste very tomato-y! There were also purple buns that were made from poi which is mashed taro root. They looked weird but tasted good.

After supper, there was a stage show with dances from around Polynesia, which includes Hawaii, New Zealand, Samoa, and Tahiti. It was very entertaining and the costuming was really colourful, and different for each dance. The Samoan Fire Dancer was definitely a crowd favourite. It was a very enjoyable evening.

One morning down by the beach in front of Jo's condo, they were doing some filming for *Hawaii Five-O*. What amazed me was the number of trailers and vehicles that were set up, and how quickly they were hauled in and hauled away again. There was a crowd of people watching, but I didn't go down. I was content to see the commotion from the balcony.

Jo and I swam in the pool a couple of times, but preferred to go in the ocean. And every Friday night there is a fireworks display. We had gone out for supper and almost missed it, but caught the last half of it from the marina. It was great.

Would I do it again?

I don't know. Maybe? I usually don't return to destinations I've already visited because there are so many other places to see, but Hawaii was so wonderful, I just might. As Jo always says,

"Hawaii is the only place in the world that everyone is sad to leave."

#56 - Go in a Submarine

January 19th

Atlantis Adventures runs a submarine tour just down the beach from Jo's condo. It's not cheap but as a once-in-a-lifetime thing, I figured it was worth it.

You meet at the pier and a boat picks you up and takes you out to the dive zone where the sub is waiting. The Atlantis submarine is about 30 m (100 ft) long and can hold up to 64 passengers.

Once you're on the sub, you descend down quite a vertical staircase (more like a ladder) into the seating area. The windows are round and because our tour was only at half capacity, we each had a window to ourselves. The ocean was a beautiful aquamarine blue.

The sub runs on batteries, that run the length of the sub, and which we were actually sitting above. They are charged each night and use only half their charge for a full day of tours. There's also an emergency battery system that can last another 24 hours. The tour is about an hour and 45 minutes long and zigzags around the 10-acre dive site.

The sub goes down 30 m (100 ft). The company sank an

airliner wreck, a shipwreck and some other things in the water to attract sea life—basically, a man-made reef.

At first, we didn't see a lot, but then things picked up. We saw a whitetip reef shark, a green sea turtle, an eel, yellow tangs as well as other kinds of fish, and my favourite: a white spotted eagle ray. I loved watching the ray swim—it was like an underwater bird flying in slow motion.

The time went by quickly, and soon we were resurfacing and loading back onto the transfer boat to go back to the pier. On the way back, we were lucky enough to pass a pod of spinner dolphins who leapt out of the water and spun around before going under again. Bonus!

Would I do it again?

I wouldn't do the same tour again, but I might go on a submarine tour in a different location.

#57 - Go on a Cruise

January 25th

After a week of relaxing in Waikiki, Jo and I boarded the *Pride of America*, a Norwegian Cruise Line ship that does a one-week cruise around the Hawaiian Islands. Jo had done it before, but it had been quite a while ago, so she was happy to join me.

Given my previous experiences with scuba diving and tandem parachuting, I was a little worried about seasickness, but my friend Gerry told me to stop at a drugstore before the cruise and buy Bonine tablets. She cruises a lot and also gets motion sick, so I figured she knew what she was talking about. I took one tablet each night at bedtime, starting the night before the cruise and never had any problems.

Embarking was a pretty smooth process, especially considering the number of people lined up to get on. The ship can hold up to 2500 passengers! That was amazing to me, but I checked and that's actually below the average capacity of cruise ships. Crazy!

There were 15 decks and we were on the eighth. We had a room with a balcony which cost more, but was worth it. When we opened the door to our room, the first thing we saw was that there was only one bed. I guess the cruise line assumed we were partners, not just friends. But the cool thing is that the large bed is actually just two smaller beds pushed together, so Jo got hold of the room steward and he said he would get the bed situation rectified. We went for a walk around the ship and when we got back there were now two smaller beds with a nightstand between them.

The ship is huge! At least it seemed like that to a newbie like me. It's 260 m (850 ft) long, has two pools, four hot tubs, six dining places where you can eat for free—it's included in the cost of the cruise—and seven specialty places where you pay extra to eat. I was amazed at how full the specialty dining places were. Call me cheap, but I just didn't get why anyone would *pay* to eat somewhere when there were other places you could eat for free! To each their own, I guess. My favourite things? The pretzel buns and the ice cream machine in the main cafeteria, the cheese fries at the fifties diner, and the appetizers in the main dining room—one evening I had a meal of just appetizers. But all the food was good—which would explain the poundage I gained on the cruise.

There was also a large theatre where there was entertainment of some kind each night. We saw two music-and-dance shows, a comedian, and a musical group. We thought the comedian was the best. There were also quite a few bars, but neither of us is a heavy drinker, so that wasn't a big attraction.

There was a video arcade, a library, an internet café—you had to pay for internet access—a fitness centre, ping pong tables, and a walking/jogging track. Jo and I walked the track a couple of times.

And of course, there were shops. I bought postcards of each of the islands we would be visiting to send to my mom. I also bought a cute nylon bag with a little holder bag attached to it. When the larger bag is stuffed into the holder, it fits in your purse or pocket. I love practical souvenirs.

Other than macadamia nuts, the only other souvenir I bought was a purple T-shirt that showed the Hawaiian Islands and the travel path the cruise takes. From Oahu we travelled to Maui, then to Hawaii ("The Big Island"), then around to the other side of Hawaii, then to Kauai, then along the Na Pali coast (the northern coast of Kauai), and back to Oahu. We left on Saturday evening and returned the following Saturday morning. The ship mostly travels through the night.

Our first stop was Kahului on Maui, where we spent two days. I was hoping to get a photograph of at least one new bird on each island, so I decided to go for a walk from the port. Easier said than done. There was a long fenced-in maze you had to follow to get away from the port, including checkpoints along the way. I was sure that one of the many turns would take me to a lever that I'd have to push to get a piece of cheese before I could continue on! I had my camera over my shoulder and the guy at the last checkpoint asked me what I was going to take pictures of.

"Birds," I replied.

"Oh, we don't have any birds here." That's what all non-birders say, and they are always wrong.

I wandered around and was beginning to think I was going to get skunked, but then in a large tree next to an insurance office, I spied not one, but two, new birds. Score!

"Did you find any birds?" the guard asked when I returned.

"I did. You have to remember that even Mynah birds are new for me," I told him. Mynah birds are extremely common on the islands.

"Well, come back this evening and there'll be a thousand of them in this tree right here."

"See? You do have birds," I said with a smile, then headed into the maze to get back to the ship.

The next day Jo and I caught a shuttle to the mall to check it out. I'm not much of a shopper, but Jo loves her "retail therapy." There were also excursions you could take, but we hadn't signed up for any on Maui. We found that all the excursions were pretty pricey. We did discover that there were also local companies that offered tours, and if I ever did it again, I would check those out ahead of time.

The first port on Hawaii was Hilo, on the eastern side of the island. It was there that we did our only excursion—to the Hawaii Tropical Botanical Gardens. So beautiful. I *heard* a lot of birds, but couldn't see them in the dense foliage for the life of me. But just walking the paths in this tropical garden was amazing. My favourite plants were the chocolate orchids. They had small flowers that really did smell like chocolate! I could have spent all day wandering around the garden, but unfortunately we only had about an hour and a half before we had to be back on the bus to return to the ship.

We didn't dock at Kona, on the other side of Hawaii, but anchored off-shore and took tenders into shore. Tenders are small boats that shuttle passengers to the port and back all day.

After Jo and I returned to the ship, I was relaxing out on the balcony when I looked down and saw a hammerhead shark!

"Jo! Come here! Quick!" I called. I wanted to make sure I wasn't imagining it. Thankfully, it stuck around long enough for Jo to see it, too. Of course, I didn't have my camera at the time, but grabbed it and hoped the shark would return.

"How cool was that!" I gushed.

We waited and watched for it to return, but no luck. But then a huge barracuda swam by! It must have been at least five feet long. I did get photos of *it*. I found out later from the Hawaiian Fisheries Department that the crew feeds the fish, and that's why they show up there.

Kauai is the rainiest of the islands, but the only rain we got was when the ship was travelling along the Na Pali coast.

Would I do it again?

I'm not sure. Jo says I should at least try an Alaskan cruise before I make up my mind. I prefer going to one place and getting to know it, rather than visiting a bunch of different places for only a short time each. But we'll see.

#58 - Go Parasailing

February 3rd

My last adventure in Hawaii was parasailing. Jo insisted that I wait until after the cruise, "just in case." There was a booking office at the marina that was just a short walk from the condo. They take people up in pairs, so I asked Jo if she wanted to join me.

"Not a chance, but I'll come along for the ride and take pictures." Deal. The woman in the office said they would pair me up with someone. Great!

We were told to arrive half an hour before our scheduled departure time to fill out the necessary waivers. Because of my scuba and parachuting experiences—stomach-wise—I took a Bonine pill the night before.

There were eight of us, plus the driver and the guide. It was a little choppy going out to the spot where we would be parasailing, so I was glad I'd taken the Bonine.

I was the last to go up, which was good because it gave me a chance to see how it worked. Since I didn't have a partner, a young woman who had gone before got to go again (for free) so I could go.

We all had to put harnesses on. Then when it was your turn to go, you went to the back of the boat and got hooked up to the parasail. I thought we'd have to start in the water, so I was happy to see that it would be a (relatively) dry take-off and landing.

There were three lengths of line you could choose—from 90 to 300 m (300 to 1000 ft). The longer the line, the longer the ride—3 to 10 min.—and the higher you went—45 to 150 m (150 to 500 ft)—and of course, the more it cost. But since this was likely going to be a once-in-a-lifetime experience, I chose the longest line.

Once you're strapped in, the boat speeds up and pretty soon you are gently lifted into the air. It reminded me a lot of the lift off in the hot air balloon. I loved it! We had a great view of the shoreline, and we chatted about where we were from and why we chose to try parasailing. The young woman was from California and had come to Oahu with her co-worker for the weekend, and they were packing in as many activities as they could before they had to fly home that night.

At the end of the ride, the operator reels in the line and you start to descend. They took us right down to water level—and then dunked us in up to our waists—before lifting us up again. A little chilly, but kind of refreshing. Then we landed on the back of the boat, where we took off from, and got unhooked.

Would I do it again?

Maybe? It was awesome, but I'm not sure if it would be as awesome a second time.

#59 - Play Blackjack at a Casino

February 8th

I go to a casino once in a while, but only to play the slots. I've *seen* the blackjack tables but have never been brave enough to try them—until today. My friend, Marilyn (my belly dancing, lawn bowling friend), had also only played the slots before, and agreed to join me.

I picked Marilyn up and we drove out to the Dakota Dunes Casino, about 20 minutes from Saskatoon. Once inside, we casually strolled by the blackjack tables—then chickened out and decided to "warm up" on the slots first.

After a $20 warm-up, it was time to find a table for real this time. We casually strolled by again, checking out what the lowest minimum bet was at each table. $10? Too rich for my blood. $2? Well, seeing as there was no $1 table, it would have to do.

We explained to the dealer, a young woman, that we'd never played before, and she told us there were computer blackjack terminals that were only $1 minimum bets, if we wanted to try that. She was just finishing her shift on the table and even took us over and showed us where the machines were and how to play.

We tried, but the machines were kind of lame. If I'm going to play a machine, I'll stick to a slot machine. So, we headed back to the table and each bought $20 in chips, explaining to the new dealer that we'd never done this before.

I *understand* how to play blackjack—but that doesn't mean I'm good at it. The first hand, I lost. Second hand was a push—the dealer and I tied, so I didn't lose but I didn't win either. Third hand, I lost. Fourth hand, I lost. Fifth hand, I lost. I was beginning to see a pattern. Sixth hand, I had 20, and was sure I was finally going to win! Nope. The dealer got 21. Seventh hand, I lost. Eighth hand—I WON!—because the dealer busted (went over 21) so we all won. But hey, a win is a win! Ninth, tenth, eleventh and twelfth hands, I lost, and I was done. Losing $20 on the slots usually takes me at least half an hour. Losing $20 on blackjack took less than 10 minutes. Bummer.

Marilyn did better than I did, but after another 10 minutes she cashed out her remaining $10 and we headed back to the slots.

Would I do it again?

No. Slots are way more fun. Even if you do win at blackjack, there's no flashing lights and bells and whistles. That's half the fun of winning! "Woohoo! I won $3!" Who cares that I spent $10 to win it. "Look at the pretty lights!"

#60! - Get a Tattoo

February 14th

Just like I knew from the beginning what my first adventure would be, I knew my last one would be to get a tattoo. On the recommendation of my friend, Tanya, I went to Tantrix Body Art in the middle of November for a consultation. I wanted to go in early enough to make sure I could get an appointment for February 14th, the last day I would be 60. Before I went, I made a sketch of what I had in mind. I wanted something simple, that I could see on myself without contortions or a mirror, and that would remind me of the great year I had. I decided on a bracelet just above my right wrist, with #60 in the center and coloured chevron stripes to make the band.

I met with Francisco and explained why I was getting a tattoo. I showed him my design and explained it didn't have to be exactly like that, as long as it was a colourful bracelet with #60 on it. He took a copy of my design and said it should be fine. We set the appointment for February 14th, and I was on my way.

I was so excited when Valentine's Day finally arrived. People had warned me that getting a tattoo would really hurt, but I have a pretty high pain tolerance, so I wasn't worried about it.

I stopped at 7-11 and got a Slurpee, as they suggested in their pre-tattoo instructions—to keep your blood sugar up while you're getting the tattoo—then off to Tantrix I went. I arrived 15 minutes early. Did I mention how excited I was?

Francisco cleaned and shaved the area above my wrist where the tattoo would go, then we chose the colours of ink—black for the outline, and purple, orange, green, yellow, blue and red for the chevron stripes, alternating with blank ones. Nice! He laid the cut-out pattern of the tattoo on my arm to transfer the design. It didn't line up right at first, so Francisco wiped that one off and adjusted the design—in order for the #60 to be centered and the ends of the band to be centered on the other side of my arm, one band had to be longer than the other. He transferred the new pattern onto my arm and it lined up perfectly.

Francisco picked up the tattoo gun, which reminded me of an engraving device. It was time to start. Suddenly a voice popped into my head. *Oh no! This is really going to hurt and you're going to jerk your arm away and you'll have a really messed up tattoo and it will probably get infected and . . .*

"Hello, Ennaid. Long time no hear," I silently replied. "I am doing this. Now zip it!" I turned my head away, gritted my teeth, and Francisco began.

After a few seconds, I turned back again. "Really? That's it? Everybody kept telling me how much it was going to hurt!"

Francisco smiled. "A lot of people exaggerate."

No kidding! It wasn't bad at all. Sort of like a cross between a burn—like I've gotten many times pulling something out of the oven—and a small continuous shock. I relaxed.

He did the outline first, then filled in the colours. While he worked, we chatted. I learned he builds and flies remote control model airplanes in his spare time. He asked about some of the other things I had done before this one, and when I mentioned I had started learning German, he told me that he had taken a tattoo course in Germany and had learned some German, too. We went back and forth teaching each other the words we knew.

I didn't keep track of how long it took to do the actual tattoo, but I'd guess about an hour. We had such a great conversation, the time flew by. When it was done, Francisco put a clear bandage over the tattoo. It was like sticky plastic wrap, but thicker. He also gave me another one to replace it with, and a page of after-care instructions.

Would I do it again?

Nope. Some people also told me that tattoos were addicting—once I got one, I'd be back for more. But no, I'm good. This one is special and I'm really glad I got it, but it's all I want.

Update on #1 (one year)

February 15th

I figured when I shaved my head, that I wouldn't have to worry about getting a haircut for the whole year. Well, I turned 61 today, and couldn't wait to get it cut! Who knew my hair would grow so fast! Before Rachel cut it—Tracy was away—I pulled out a ruler and asked her to measure it.

"Almost seven inches long," she reported. (18 cm)

"Wow! That's crazy," I exclaimed. "Now please, *cut it!"*

Epilogue

February 15

Happy 61st birthday to me!

What a great year that was! I'm so glad I turned 60 in 2019 and not 2020. It would be pretty hard to come up with things I've never done before—without leaving my house! Nasty COVID-19. But it did give me time to finish writing this book, so there's that.

Not that anyone is going to want to read it.

"Oh, Ennaid ..."

As I was saying, I had a blast! There were definite highlights and a few lowlights. There were things I was happy to do once and leave it at that, and things I will continue to do. And there were surprises. A lot of surprises.

I think my favourite thing was shaving my head (#1). It's something I always wanted to do and it was a fantastic way to kick off this whole adventure. It makes me smile even now.

There was only one thing I actually *regretted* doing, and that was eating haggis (#34). You might have thought that I also regretted doing the tandem parachute jump (#35), but no. It was terrifying, and I would never ever do it again, but at least I have bragging rights for surviving it. There is nothing to brag about for surviving haggis.

The most surprising thing had to be the nudist camp (#38). The phrase "don't knock it 'til you try it" should be the motto for nudism. I never would have imagined how comfortable I would feel. Body shape and size is just not an issue. It's a totally different mindset, that's for sure. I'm actually looking forward to returning.

The things I will continue to do are my daily German lessons on Duolingo (#6), and playing the trombone (#29). I'm playing 3rd trombone in our local community jazz band now. *Und ich lerne gerne Deutsch.*

The two things I liked so much I plan to take them up, are lawn bowling (#15), and playing the harp (#13). I'll start out with a small 26-string harp, but would love to own and play a full-size one someday.

I discovered volunteer opportunities that I want to continue as well: the Nature Conservancy of Canada (#14), the Saskatchewan Jazz Festival (#24) and Ronald MacDonald House (#45). It's great when helping out can be so much fun!

I even expanded my knowledge of some other cultures and religions by attending Folkfest (#33), a pow wow (#46), Buddhist meditation (#48) and by touring a mosque (#50). All great experiences.

So, looking back, how did I make out on my list? Well, I did 43 out of the original 100 things. Not bad. That means I came up with 17 other things that I hadn't even considered before, like going on a paddlewheeler (#21) and tenpin bowling (#49). If I've learned anything in the last year, it's that when opportunities come knocking, throw on a robe and answer the door! With a couple of new benchmarks—"It can't possibly be scarier than jumping out of an airplane!" and "It can't possibly taste worse than haggis!"—I'm excited to see what might be next. After all, I didn't even cross off *half* of the original list—there are still a lot of new adventures out there.

Sixty-one is not old, right?

The 60 Things I Did

1. Shaved my head
2. Floated in a sensory deprivation tank
3. Got my eyebrows threaded
4. Visited the Remai Modern Art Gallery
5. Got an acupuncture treatment
6. Started learning German
7. Tried axe throwing
8. Tried scuba diving
9. Went to a Rush game
10. Got my hair dyed
11. Got a manicure
12. Took a belly dancing class
13. Played the harp
14. Volunteered with the Nature Conservancy of Canada
15. Tried lawn bowling
16. Went on a hot air balloon ride
17. Visited the Yukon
18. Visited Alaska
19. Traveled in a truck camper
20. Drank a Sourtoe Cocktail
21. Went on a paddlewheeler
22. Panned for gold
23. Rode a Ninebot
24. Volunteered at the Jazz Festival

25. Visited the Tunnels of Moose Jaw
26. Got a personalized license plate
27. Paddled a dragon boat
28. Tried folk dancing
29. Started learning to play the trombone
30. Got a henna tattoo
31. Went skinny dipping
32. Smoked marijuana
33. Went to Folkfest
34. Ate haggis
35. Did a tandem parachute jump
36. Celebrated my birthday in the summer
37. Drank a martini
38. Attended a nudist camp
39. Attended a sing-along movie
40. Tried paddleboarding
41. Composed a choir piece
42. Composed a handbell piece
43. Visited the (2nd) biggest tree in Saskatchewan
44. Visited the Crooked Trees
45. Volunteered at Ronald McDonald House
46. Attended a pow wow
47. Ate smoked cheese
48. Attended a Buddhist meditation class
49. Tried tenpin bowling
50. Toured a mosque
51. Visited the Canadian Light Source synchrotron
52. Got a reflexology treatment
53. Drove a snowmobile
54. Tried downhill skiing
55. Visited Hawaii

56. Went on a submarine
57. Went on a cruise
58. Went parasailing
59. Played blackjack at a casino
60. Got a tattoo

Postscript

Thank you for reading my book.
If you enjoyed it, please spread the word. I appreciate it.

If you would like to see photos of my adventures, check out:
my website: https://dianneyoung.ca (My 60 Things)
or
my 60 Things Facebook page:
https://www.facebook.com/mysixtythings
or
my Twitter feed: https://twitter.com/writerdyoung (#60things)

Acknowledgements

Thanks to my wonderful editor, Paula Jane Remlinger. If you don't like the way I wrote something, it's probably because I ignored her suggestion.

And thanks to all the friends who joined me on my adventures—Amber, Cathrin, Betty Lou, Barb, Ross, Erin, Murray, Debbie P., Dave, Karen, Lynn, Marilyn, Pat, Candice, Myrna, Adrienne (and all the members of our dragon boat team), Yvonne, Lianne, Brittney, Sheila, Diane, Owen, Rachelle, Rylee, Beth, Bette, Chris, Christian, Debbie W., Jeanette, Jon, Keith, Michael, Scott, Brenda, Ken, Maryann, Austin, and Jo. And thanks to Emma T. for being such a good listener. It was a great year! I'm sure there will be more adventures to come—but not five a month!

About the Author

Dianne Young has always preferred trying new things to practicing the same ones over and over—just ask her childhood piano teacher! The mantra "you never know until you try" gave Dianne the incentive to leap out of her comfort zone and prove to herself that 60's not so old after all. A mother, a writer, a birder, a widow, a retiree—Dianne lives with her dog, Posey, and her cat, Lysette, in Martensville, Saskatchewan.

You can connect with me on:

- https://dianneyoung.ca
- https://twitter.com/writerdyoung
- https://www.facebook.com/mysixtythings

Also by Dianne Young

Dear Me: The Widow Letters
If you could send a letter back in time to your newly-widowed self—that heartbroken, overwhelmed woman—what would you say?

Twenty courageous women of various ages, widowed under various circumstances, responded to that question with these heartfelt letters. They are letters of grief, of love and, most importantly, of hope.

Available at https://diannesbookstore.bigcartel.com

(Use code 60THINGS for free shipping!)

Printed in Dunstable, United Kingdom

70378932R00100